Yes, you can... ENJOY TODAY: Because this day, not someday, is the only day that matters

Copyright © 2025 by Jim Greenwood
All rights reserved.

No part of this book may be reproduced, stored in a retrieval system, or transmitted in any form or by any means—electronic, mechanical, photocopying, recording, or otherwise—without the prior written permission of the publisher, except in the case of brief quotations used in reviews or scholarly works.

A TOSSLY Institute Book

ISBN: 979-8-9990218-2-3 (eBook)
ISBN: 979-8-9990218-1-6 (Paperback)
ISBN: 979-8-9990218-0-9 (Hardcover)

For information, contact: info@tossly.com

Available at Amazon.com and bookstores everywhere

TABLE OF CONTENTS

Preface 9

Introduction 11

Have You Thought About The Arc Of Your Life? 17

Your Small Steps Are Yours To Choose 19

Your Self-Talk Is Your Constant Companion 25

Your Perspective Shapes Your Opportunities 29

Enjoy. Today. 43

Yes, There Are Problems 49

Are "Growing Up Voices" Challenging You? 55

Are The Voices Of Others Affecting You? 59

Yes, There Are Practices To Enjoy More 63
   1. A PTR Practice: Refreshes Your Moments 67
   2. A BIT Practice: Shifts Your Mindset To Enjoy Today. 77
   3. A TFM Practice: Guides You Throughout Your Day 85
   4. A W4G Practice: Becomes Your Friendly Collaborator 95
      How To Start A W4G Practice   99
   5. A Personal Strengths Practice: For Taking Small Steps ... 119

Your Thinking Adds Strength	*125*
Your Body Adds Strength	*141*
Your Emotion Adds Strength	*151*
Your Spirit Adds Strength	*167*
Time Adds Strength	*187*

Your Definition Of Words 207

You Can Stop Warring With Yourself 211

You Being You Is The Best 215

Begin—To Enjoy Today 219

Conclusion 221

Glossary Of Terms 223

List Of Quotations 229

Acknowledgements 245

About JG 247

"Jim Greenwood is a very wise, generous, and successful man. He has lots to teach us not only about business but about life."

—Morton Schapiro,
Former President of Northwestern University and Williams College

*When you are ready,
the beginning will appear.*

PREFACE

Enjoy Today is a powerful companion for you if you want to feel more grounded, fulfilled, and present in your everyday life. Instead of offering quick fixes or overwhelming self-help formulas, this book gently guides readers to recognize the value of small steps and daily choices. It teaches that you don't need a perfect life to enjoy it—you just need to notice what's already good and build from there.

Through approachable tools like the BIT practice (See The Best In Today), guided self-talk, and perspective-shaping strategies, readers learn how to reduce stress, calm worry, and reconnect with their inner strength. *Enjoy Today* shows you how to pause, reflect, and shift your attention in ways that lead to more joy, better decision-making, and a deeper sense of self-worth.

Whether you're navigating change, dealing with burnout, or simply seeking more meaning in your routines, *Enjoy Today* offers you practical ways to create emotional balance and forward momentum. You'll come away with a renewed sense of clarity, the ability to guide your thoughts, and a deepened appreciation for the everyday moments that matter most. This book reminds you that today isn't just a placeholder—it's the most important place to begin.

> "The best time to plant a tree was twenty years ago. The second best time is now."
> **—Chinese Proverb**

INTRODUCTION

Footsteps on warm earth,
Each step a story unfolding,
Today shapes my path.

IN CASE YOU WONDERED

My friend Les asked me, "What was your journey like before Enjoy Today?"

I paused.

Then, almost without thinking, I said, "Busy." I'd been spending most of my time acquiring, and working hard to bring more of what I wanted into my life. Confidence, relationships, family, friends, health, money. I fully experienced the ups and downs of both momentum and emotions. I enjoyed the ups (at least for a bit), and I worried about the downs (for a bit longer).

The philosophy of Enjoy Today hadn't yet occurred to me. Looking back, I wish I had known about it. Looking forward, I'd like to share with you some of its lessons and some of the ways you can choose to Enjoy Today—this one day.

That said . . .

WHAT IS ENJOY TODAY?

Enjoy Today is a book, but it's also a philosophy that recognizes enjoyment enriches our lives in ways both conscious and unconscious. It's not about eliminating problems, stress, overwhelm, or worry. Why? Because we are all human. It's about acknowledging their reality and then taking moments to strengthen and guide yourself, regardless of the problem.

Everyone will have good days and bad days, and finding moments to enjoy, even on the bad days, provides meaningful benefits. The practices of Enjoy Today will help you develop the ability to see and reap those benefits. Why? Because it is also human to enjoy.

You may have heard there are two types of power: hard power and soft power.

Hard power is the hammer.

Soft power is the feather.

Enjoy Today is soft power.

Enjoy Today offers no one way, only your way.

With Enjoy Today, you can become a master of the feather.

Introduction

THE POWER LIES IN *SMALL STEPS*

I've come to understand that life isn't about those rare, dramatic moments of triumph you often see celebrated. It's about the moments when you decide to try again, change course, move through the difficulty, make that phone call, appreciate what you have instead of complaining, or calm yourself even when stress is building.

The power to do so lies in taking *small steps*. *Small steps* connect you with your moments and the now of your life, reminding you to live fully—not someday, but right now. With your "end in mind," they shape and guide the life you desire, one step, one day at a time.

Through *small steps*, you can become whatever you want: an athlete, a teacher, a social worker, rich or famous—whatever calls you or you stumble upon. *Small steps* will help you learn from those who inspire you—to be sweet or tough, work hard, read everything, breathe, stay in touch, or whatever feels right for your chosen path.

Over the years, this phrase kept coming to me: The Truth Of *Small Steps*—Lead Yourself (it has also been Love Yourself). I shortened this phrase to TOSSLY. When I shared these thoughts with friends, one person asked, *"Why is TOSSLY so focused on the self? 'Lead yourself?' 'Love yourself?'"* I had a simple answer: You can only change yourself. You can't change anyone else.

YES, YOU CAN ENJOY TODAY

Enjoy Today is for you. Perhaps it'll also be for your friend, your sister, your brother, or your neighbor, but right now, it's for you.

Yes, Enjoy Today is for you. I acknowledge that hearing your true self is more complex and nuanced than ever, and there are a million voices out there, each with their own opinions on what you could do, should do, or should not do.

In this book, you will find practices to guide you whenever and wherever you choose. What works for you and what you choose to work on will depend on where you are in life and what makes sense to you. If you don't want to or need to now, someday you will. Taking *small steps* is always within your reach.

Know this:

- ➢ Your perspective and direction will differ if you're twenty-five, forty-five, or seventy-five. Different genders will interpret concepts differently.
- ➢ Involving trusted friends in your steps will be beneficial. With the input of others, your life will be richer and fuller.
- ➢ Enjoy Today is meant to help, not to replace or override medical or professional advice.

Enjoy Today is an overview of well-known paths in life, not an in-depth exploration of any one of them. For that, there are excellent resources available in any area you are interested in

Introduction

exploring more deeply. Listen to and learn from the ones that make sense to you.

At the end of this book, you'll find a glossary of terms for the words I use and a list of quotations that have motivated me. If you'd like to know more about me and where I'm coming from, you'll also find a short section, "About JG," with a bit about where and how these philosophies developed.

This is your book. Talk to it. Write in the margins.

If you have any questions or comments, please email me at jim@tossly.com.

YOU HAVE A SPECIAL GIFT—AND YOU CAN USE IT

It's a gift you receive every day, whether you like it or not. You can't return it, postpone it, or save it for later, and it's a gift that becomes what you make of it.

What is it?

You've probably guessed: It's today.

And while it's impossible to predict the exact number of these gifts you have left, you know this: It's a finite number that slips away one by one, making each day matter.

So perhaps the most important question you can ask isn't how many days you have left, but rather how to spend the one you have right now—to enjoy and benefit from this one day.

"None of us, including me, can do great things without others. But we can all do small things, with great love, and together, we can do something wonderful."
—Mother Teresa

HAVE YOU THOUGHT ABOUT THE ARC OF YOUR LIFE?

Your Today is on an ARC of life. Each of us has one. It's a personal storyline that has a beginning, a middle, and an end—and you are the main character. Over time, its stages and phases significantly influence a plot where you develop and/or decline.

Where you are on this ARC matters because it shapes how you see the world, how you make your choices, and, ultimately, how you enjoy your days. Its stages are broad and general, and they overlap, providing the "big picture" for your thoughts, feelings, and actions.

Your ARC begins at birth. From this time and roughly into middle age, you **A**ccumulate education, relationships, resources, careers, children, and other things. In this stage, you work hard to find your who, what, where, and how.

Then you move into **R**ecognition—milestone birthdays, personal evaluation of successes and failures, kids leaving home, and retirement; this stage generally lasts into the mid-sixties.

Then, finally, you reach **C**onsolidation—considering how to spend your remaining days, seeing your body change, grandchildren, legacy, preparing your estate, and taking care of other important business. This stage usually starts in the mid- to late sixties.

Everyone is different, but the ARC remains the same.

Does this ring a bell? Where do you think you are on your ARC of life?

I've thought that those in the **R**ecognition and **C**onsolidation stages would gain the greatest benefits from Enjoy Today, but I've been told emphatically that those in the **A**cquisition stage can benefit from it as well. Come to think about it, I wish I had known these things when I was younger.

Whatever stage you're in, the truth is that today is the only day you can see things more clearly, enjoy what you have, or seek something else that will move you forward toward more of what you want.

> "Start where you are. Use what you have.
> Do what you can."
> **—Arthur Ashe**

YOUR SMALL STEPS ARE YOURS TO CHOOSE

Small steps are a process, not a miracle.

Think about it. When was the last time you accomplished something meaningful? Maybe you bounced back from a setback, strengthened a relationship, built a new habit, or navigated a particularly tough week. How did you get there? Wasn't it, in reality, a collection of small steps, small actions, that led to the result?

Falling in love, having kids, or building a home, a business, or a career doesn't happen overnight. It's always about the often unnoticed *small steps* that move you closer to what you want—to accept a challenge, to overcome it, and to learn from it. Big achievements and lasting relationships may steal the spotlight, but the real work, the real magic, is in the *small steps* that move you toward what you desire.

Wherever you are on the ARC of your life, whether everything finally falls into place or inspiration strikes in a single moment, progress always unfolds through *small steps*—thinking, feeling, overcoming doubts, and moving forward with confidence.

Small steps make big choices feel possible and progress inevitable. They don't remove the need for decisions, directions, or breakthroughs. Instead, they prepare you for them and create the foundations for movement in your direction of growth. Sometimes, your steps will be one after another; sometimes, they'll move backward and forward. Most times, you'll find yourself being open to several possible steps before choosing the ones to actually take.

Some call them baby steps, incremental steps, or even miniature milestones. Whatever you call them, they are your foundational path to decisions and capturing the moments of enjoying today, and they can be called on whenever needed. These steps might go unnoticed, but they are the very building blocks of progress.

So why aren't *small steps* used more purposefully?

Maybe they are overlooked because, in their smallness, they seem unimportant. Maybe, overwhelmed by the pressures of daily life, we are focused on the bigger picture. Or maybe *small steps* take time and need guidance to build on one another, and it can be challenging to see past the particular moment to the next *small steps* ahead?

Small steps aren't loud or forceful but rather a quiet mingling of personal strengths and direction that gives you confidence, clarity, and momentum. The anatomy of a *small step* is a fluid blend of idea, situation, review, selection, staging, implementation, and acknowledgment—all happening simultaneously to guide your move and to prepare you for the next one.

> The truth of moving forward is to get started.
> The truth to getting started is small steps.
> The truth of making progress is to keep going.
> The truth to keep going is small steps.

Many will suggest the next steps for you to take, but only you can decide. You have to take your own *small steps*; no one can take them for you. You are your advocate, your guide, and your destination.

Find your next *small step* by tuning in to yourself and truly listening to what you're saying. Some close their eyes, take a deep breath, then take their step; others simply put one foot in front of the other, and still others start shifting the words they use from *"I can't"* to *"I will."*

Your first step might be asking yourself, *"Am I enjoying what I'm doing?" "Is there a change I want to make?" "In which areas do I need to focus?"* Among the first steps may be unlearning habits of the past by asking, *"Am I justifying or defending what's unhelpful? Why?" "Am I avoiding needed change out of comfort, fear, or routine?" "What would my future self thank me for unlearning today?"*

Enjoy Today

> When you take the easy ones,
> the tough ones become easier.

Power lies in fully embracing the present moment, and s*mall steps* are always taken in the present moment, in the now of life. They allow you to build your ability in achievable increments, and importantly, this enables you to take them whenever you choose.

The truth is:

- All *small steps* are sized to be achievable.
- All *small steps* happen in the now.
- Taken one by one, *small steps* are manageable and build momentum.
- *Small steps* guide all forward (or backward) movement in your life.
- *Small steps* are what lead to and away from giant steps.
- Celebrating each *small step* is a real piece of progress.
- *Small steps* can lead to success or failure. Success brings smiles; failure brings lessons.
- Like all things in life, *small steps* are affected by luck and timing.
- *Small steps* always take time, but that's OK because overnight success is a myth.

- *Small steps* become more apparent and more meaningful in hindsight.

ASK YOURSELF

- Were there *small steps* that became turning points in your life?
- In moments of stress, which steps do you call on?
- In moments of opportunity, which steps will be called on?
- Are there steps you have been hesitant to take?
- What steps might you take today?

> "You don't have to see the whole staircase;
> just take the first step."
> **—Martin Luther King Jr**

YOUR SELF-TALK IS YOUR CONSTANT COMPANION

Perspective leads to self-talk.
Self-talk shapes your perspective.

Have you noticed your mind is a nonstop storyteller, weaving tales that shape and color your reality? This internal narrative—your self-talk—is the invisible architect of your world, whether offering soothing conversation or internal conflict and argument. Taking it for granted is a mistake.

With words, phrases, and tones shaping the theme of self-talk, every silent script is sculpting your thoughts, emotions, and actions. The truth is, your self-talk is guiding your *small steps,* constantly telling you what you're enjoying and what you're stressed about. It's evaluating your past, creating your future, and guiding you toward or away from what you want.

Think you're just a passive audience? Think again. You're the author, editor, and publisher of this, your personal bestseller. The chapters you revisit become the plot of your life, influencing your every decision, reaction, and belief.

Do you ever stop and listen to the stories you tell yourself in the privacy of your mind? Of course you do. How much time do you spend listening to your opportunities and next steps, and how much time do you spend listening to your worries? Both will come and go, and both have meaning in your life.

That said, getting stuck in worry can be exhausting and make enjoying difficult. Do you share your worries with yourself first, and maybe take too much time to get to the opportunities? Do you tell yourself about opportunities and perhaps not take action on them? Does the same worry continually resurface?

The truth is:

- You can advocate for yourself in your self-talk.
- You are, and will become, your self-talk.
- Listening to your self-talk is the first step in how you choose to use it.
- Self-talk gives you a private place to listen to and refine ideas.
- What you say to yourself is often subconsciously communicated to others.

Your Self-Talk Is Your Constant Companion

- If self-talk is directing you in the direction you choose, keep listening.
- If you want to change your self-talk, you can.
- Overwriting the negativity is like muting an annoying commercial.
- You can shape your self-talk with the practices of Enjoy Today, such as TFM, BIT, TPR, and W4G.
- Writing gives you an extraordinary power in scripting self-talk.

How your self-talk speaks to you has taken years to develop, and if you want to change it, it may take time. However, your self-talk is yours to develop. In W4G (Writing 4 Growth), you'll find principles and practices to help you listen to your self-talk, shape it, and take action on it, guiding what you say to yourself toward more of what you want and less of what you don't want.

ASK YOURSELF

- Are you shaping your self-talk, or is it shaping you?
- Would you like to be better at shaping it?
- What would you add to your script?
- What would you remove?

Enjoy Today

"The most important conversation you'll ever have is the one you have with yourself."
—David Goggins

YOUR PERSPECTIVE SHAPES YOUR OPPORTUNITIES

The truth of personal perspective is clear...
You are the only person who can change yours.

Is there something you want to see differently?

You get to choose your self-talk. You decide which small steps to take. And in that same way, you hold the power to shape your perspective—one thought, one moment at a time.

Are there areas where you want greater success, connection, creativity, or balance? Shifting your perspective, beginning in your self-talk, is the place to begin—and only you can shift it.

Many resist changing their perspectives. However, if your current perspectives lead to recurring worries or feelings of stagnation, it may be worth considering a change. It can be very helpful to think about these four small manageable parts of all perspectives:

- ➤ **SIDES** represent the different viewpoints available to you in any given situation.

- ➤ **MIDDLES** depict where all paths live and *small steps* are taken.

- ➤ **BEGINNINGS** express that wherever you are now is the place to start.

- ➤ **WORDS** will always act as powerful tools in shaping your perspectives.

ASK YOURSELF

- ➤ Do you see the glass half empty or half full?
- ➤ Is it better to ask for permission or forgiveness?
- ➤ Is it better to focus on the details or the big picture?

When you answer these questions, imagine that you're wearing glasses with a unique tint. The colors represent your life experiences, current circumstances, cultural background, and personal beliefs.

These metaphorical lenses shape how each of us perceives and feels about the world around us. The tints become powerful personal guides, constantly shaping our perspective and interpretation of reality. In essence, your outlook becomes a self-fulfilling prophecy, influencing your life and your interactions with others.

We see the world through our unique lenses. This explains why two people, even with similar backgrounds, can see the same situation, the same "truths," in completely different ways.

The not-so-hidden power of personal perspective lies in taking *small steps* over time to enhance your life experience. It offers you the ability to focus on what you need and wish to bring into your life. *Is there something you'd like to bring into your life?*

TWO "SIDES" CONTRIBUTE TO YOUR PERSPECTIVES (CONSIDER THEM DESTINATIONS)

> "Today, I will see more of what I want and
> less of what I don't want."
> **—Abraham Hicks**

Every perspective has two non-binary "sides." These sides are on the same spectrum, and they're interdependent: one cannot exist without the other. One side defines the other, and both sides have benefits. Being on either side is normal. For example, sadness or frustration is an appropriate response when there is loss or delay, yet happiness still exists. Challenges test our limits, but opportunities nevertheless remain. Each side is always there, and each is intricately involved with the other.

Picture these "sides" on a seesaw where each side carries weight—sometimes heavy, sometimes light—and movement depends on the shifting balance between them. When one side lifts, the other naturally dips, just as positive and negative, opposition and acceptance, and beginnings and endings all take turns shaping our experience.

Balance, then, doesn't mean keeping the seesaw perfectly still; it means learning to adjust and finding steadiness in the rhythm of rising and falling. The trick lies in knowing that both sides have a role in guiding your purpose and choices.

Moving the "weight" from one side to the other can be difficult and may often take longer than you think. But the first step is lifting up the side of your choice. If you're sad, take a step that makes you happy. If you're stalled, take a step that moves you forward. If you're feeling weak, shift the weight to doing something that gives you strength or remove something that weighs you down.

What you see is what you get—

or stay away from.

Perspectives from family, friends, finances, home, or health can impact your overall outlook. They can fluctuate and add lightness or heaviness to your point of view. But the dynamic of sides remains the same, and taking *small steps*, as you can, offers the path to overall progress.

TIPS FOR ACHIEVING BALANCE

- ➢ If you're feeling down, know that you can lighten the weight.

- The past may make one side heavier, but that, too, can be lightened.
- Up is always an option when you're down.
- Raising the side you desire is a path to greater enjoyment.

ASK YOURSELF
- Which sides of your life are carrying the weight?
- Have you thought about ideas for improving balance?
- What steps have you taken to lighten the downsides?

It's worth remembering that nothing is ever as good or as bad as you think it is.

While you may be on one side looking at the other, progress toward your chosen side occurs in the "middles"—the space between the "sides."

THE "MIDDLES" ARE WHERE PROGRESS IS MADE (CONSIDER THEM PATHS)

>To reach the peaks, you have to
>go through valleys.

Middles are where the movement toward the sides happens. These "middles" are where transitions and actions occur (in life, love, at home, in habits, at work, etc.). It's where new directions begin or where old directions continue. They can be difficult and connected by many possible steps, including twists, forks, triggers, and blind spots.

Rarely, if ever, are middles straightaways. Moving forward is exciting, yet it also comes with the risk of falling behind. That's where a well-known perspective comes in: *"One step forward, two steps back."*

It is in the middle where ups and downs are encountered—as highs and lows and ebbs and flows of your thinking, emotions, and progress. Being alert to these patterns makes the necessary action more apparent, helping to ease the lows, savor the highs, and better guide your *small steps*.

Visualize these ups and downs as points above and below a straight line moving in the direction of your choice. The points above the line represent supportive and rewarding steps—such as success, progress, and confidence—while those below symbolize complex and challenging steps—like worry, self-doubt, and insecurity. Keeping the focus on the "ups" is a small yet effective step toward overcoming the "downs."

If you're not heading toward the side you want, simply turn around and adjust your perspective. The weight that will help you regain balance is the *small steps* that can be taken at any point in the middle.

Middles are full of curves that have earned their names because they represent perspectives you frequently encounter. These curves help you understand the whys and whats that are happening in your position and offer insight into the time or effort needed to move in your direction of choice.

Your Perspective Shapes Your Opportunities

For instance, bell curves show the perspectives of extremes and middles, illustrating the best and worst possible outcomes and the fact that most of the progress will be made in the "middle." Meanwhile, paradoxes remind us that two seemingly opposing things can be simultaneously true: you can have too much and too little at the same time—or be satisfied with what you have while still wanting more.

> "The middle is messy, but it's also where the magic happens."
> **—Brené Brown**

It bears repeating that life's biggest curve is the ARC of life. Every personal story has a beginning, middle, and end, and where you are on this curve will influence what you see and how you deal with it. Although this ARC is rarely considered and perhaps has never even been named, it has a significant influence on how you perceive your days.

This ARC, which I introduced at the beginning of the book, matters because it provides context for your thoughts and feelings. It shapes how you see the world, the choices you make, and, ultimately, how you enjoy your days. Though its stages are broad and general, and they will overlap, even a casual awareness of where you are on your personal ARC can help you see how it influences your perspective.

Our ARC begins at birth and lasts roughly into middle age as we **A**ccumulate—education, relationships, resources, careers, children, etc.

Then we move into **R**ecognition—milestone birthdays, evaluations of successes and failures, kids leaving home, and retirement. We generally remain in this stage into our late sixties.

Then, finally, we reach **C**onsolidation—considering how to spend our remaining days, enjoying grandchildren, thinking about our legacy, preparing our estate. This stage usually occurs from our late sixties onward.

The lessons we learn and the resources we gain in the **A**ccumulating stage of our ARC then offer valuable perspectives in **R**ecognition and **C**onsolidation.

TIPS FOR NAVIGATING MIDDLES

- Having an "end in mind" guides your steps through the middle.
- The middle is the path where *small step*s are taken.
- Middles encompass the steps from bottom to top—or top to bottom.
- Middles are like a bridge connecting one side to the other.
- Beginnings are the first steps onto that bridge.
- Endings are like stepping off the bridge on the other side.
- The middle that feels tough or boring offers valuable lessons and opportunities for growth.

ASK YOURSELF

- ➢ Are you in the middle of something?
- ➢ Which side are you moving toward?
- ➢ What steps are you taking to get there?
- ➢ What steps could you take?

When you are ready, the beginning will appear.

It's valuable to remember that whenever you are in the middle, it's just another starting point. Wherever you stand right now offers a new "beginning."

"BEGINNINGS" ARE YOURS TO CHOOSE (SEIZE EACH DAY, EACH MOMENT, AS A NEW OPPORTUNITY)

> "The beginning is the most important
> part of the work."
> **—Plato**

Picture life as a dance: whether you're moving forward or backward, the spot where you're standing is always where your next step begins. In events like games, classes, or meetings, beginnings are clear-cut and structured. In life, you dictate when something new starts. It's your call.

Viewing each moment as a beginning transforms every instant into a potential fresh start or a powerful continuation. You get to choose which way to go next, starting with a *small step* from whatever spot you're on. Right now, you can wrap up old business or initiate something new. Right now.

Approaching new beginnings may involve asking questions such as, *"What would I like to do now?" "What could I do differently?"* or *"What is my next step?"*

The mere act of contemplating these questions is a new beginning. Answering them is another *small step* to exploring a new path. No grand gestures are required; simply entertaining thoughts of change or greater enjoyment marks the start. A personal beginning is an ever-present, wide-open door. It doesn't have to be a distant, elusive concept. Your only task? To decide to step through it.

TIPS FOR BEGINNINGS

- Beginnings allow you to shape your experiences.
- You get to choose which direction to go.
- Beginning again often reveals your true motivations.
- Your willingness to take risks can also be found in beginnings.
- Beginnings are the first step that guides the next steps.

ASK YOURSELF

- Is there something you need to end?
- Is there something you've avoided beginning?

Your Perspective Shapes Your Opportunities

> Just for fun, how would you begin?

> "You may be in the middle of a chapter,
> but you can always start a new one."

Your language shapes your perspectives and is a powerful instigator (or detractor) of your beginnings. Say what you will, and know that what you say is very powerful.

"WORDS" SHAPE YOUR PERSPECTIVES (YOUR WORDS, PHRASES, AND TONES GUIDE YOU)

> "Words are the most powerful force
> available to humanity."
> **—Yehuda Berg**

You wield a potent force that can reshape reality, ignite revolutions, or mend broken hearts. Words—along with their phrases and tones—are not just sounds or scribbles; they're the architects of your thinking, the sculptors of your emotions, and your personal internal life coaches. They're always on call, ready to push, inspire, or sabotage.

The words you use to guide your thoughts, your feelings, and the ways you connect with the world are the GPS guiding your *small steps* and your path through life. And you're the programmer. Every syllable uttered or thought about is like a tiny seed planted in the fertile soil of your mind, ready to bloom into what you choose—self-doubt or self-confidence.

Think about it: Has a casual comment from another ever derailed your day? Or has a well-timed compliment propelled you to something better? These results are the raw power of language at work.

The words you say to yourself are not about positive thinking; they're the small steps to thinking more positively.

Even with all their power, words can't fully express big emotions, sensory experiences, gut feelings, or infinite or abstract concepts. How often have you seen those who have suffered a tremendous loss or are enjoying a great victory lost for words, unable to express their feelings? This inability, in the moment, to find the right words is human, favoring emotion over intellect.

Language will guide your mindset, one word or phrase at a time. Over time, instead of dwelling on *"I can't,"* ask yourself, *"How can I?"* And when doubt whispers, *"I'm not good enough,"* try replacing it with, *"I can do this."*

> Today, I will tell myself more of what
> I enjoy and less of what I don't like.

TIPS FOR USING WORDS EFFECTIVELY

- ➤ The tone you use is as important as the words themselves.
- ➤ Both positive and negative words are helpful at different times.

Your Perspective Shapes Your Opportunities

- Kind words lead to better relationships with yourself—and others.
- Repeating words gives them their power.
- Words can point you in the direction of your choice.
- Words are not good or bad; it depends on how and where you use them.
- Enjoy Today are two words to remember every day.

ASK YOURSELF

- Are you aware of the words you're telling yourself?
- Do your words match what you want in life?
- If they don't, have you thought about changing them?

> "Words are free; how you use them may cost you."
> **—Kushandwizdom**

ENJOY. TODAY.

"Enjoy life. There's plenty of time to be dead."
—**Hans Christian Andersen**

To Enjoy Today is not about forgetting yesterday, settling, or giving up on tomorrow. Instead, it's about appreciating the power of today, this one day, and letting it fuel a greater sense of contentment and purpose.

"Enjoy" means to take pleasure or find satisfaction in something, whether it's an activity, experience, or moment. It often involves a sense of happiness, appreciation, or contentment and frequently comes with a slight smile.

"Today" refers to the current day—the twenty-four-hour period in which you are presently living. It represents the time between yesterday and tomorrow. It, and only it, provides the opportunity for action, reflection, and presence.

In today's fast-paced world, you're often encouraged to chase enjoyment through achievements, money, accomplishments, and future goals. Yet, when there are problems and worries they command attention. You can forget to take a moment to recognize and enjoy what you already have.

Yes, some days will bring adversity, such as loss, setbacks, sadness, and discouragement. Enjoyment quite rightly fades or disappears in these moments and can take time to reemerge. Enjoy Today can be challenging, but it is still there, waiting to provide support.

Why find it? Because enjoying makes you feel connected to your experiences rather than distracted or overwhelmed, and it's like discovering something that's been hiding in plain sight. You're shifting your focus from what's missing to what's present.

The philosophy of Enjoy Today is not about denying life's realities, like the stresses of money and work, home and family, health and wellness, or social stress. But even in the middle of all that, you can take a moment—or find one—to notice and appreciate something you enjoy. These small moments may seem insignificant, but taken daily, they add up. They create a habit of presence. They build a foundation of contentment. They remind you that even on hard days, there's still something worth enjoying.

Building awareness of enjoyment is key, and as you cultivate this awareness, it's like finding a missing step toward what you want or need. Remember this:

- ➢ Enjoyment comes from within.
- ➢ Enjoyment can be present even when you're focused elsewhere or your days are challenging.

Enjoy. Today.

- ➢ Enjoyment isn't always loud or obvious and often hides in the quiet corners of our lives.
- ➢ Enjoyment isn't something anyone can tell you to do, you have to notice it.
- ➢ It's waiting for you to notice it.

Enjoyment means different things to different people and changes as we grow and our priorities shift. For some, it's found in their everyday lives or in the fulfillment they derive from their work. For others, it's finding greatness in their careers. Still, for others, it's nurturing relationships, being creative, serving others, finding adventure, or spending time with family.

Whatever enjoyment means to you, its benefits are well known. It creates good feelings and a positive emotional response, making you smile or want to smile and feel good in the moment. It involves experiencing a sense of appreciation while engaging in an activity, interacting with others, or even during moments of reflection.

Seeking to Enjoy Today is a meaningful activity that can add years to your life—and life to your years.

Science has shown that enjoyment brings many benefits, including improved cardiovascular health, lower blood pressure, a stronger immune system, increased social connections, and the development of stronger relationships.

Enjoying the small things helps you enjoy the bigger things, and today, whether you're taking action, seeing results, or planning for the future, is the only place you can enjoy. Today is where you

Enjoy Today

will find the extraordinary power of the present. When tomorrow arrives, it will be another today presenting its opportunity.

- Enjoyment better equips you to handle life's problems, stresses, and worries.
- Enjoyment has a positive impact on both your physical and mental health.
- Enjoyment leads to increased creativity and productivity.
- Enjoying your relationships strengthens them.
- The more you enjoy life, the more you grow and discover yourself.

ASK YOURSELF

- What would you add to this list?
- What do you enjoy doing?
- Who do you enjoy being with?
- What activities make you lose track of time?
- What small moments in your daily life make you smile?

> "The past is unchangeable, and the future is uncertain. Therefore, our focus should be on making the most of today."
> **—John Wooden**

Enjoy. Today.

Enjoying Today can take practice. In the section, Yes, There Are Practices To Enjoy More, you'll find several practices for your consideration.

> "Enjoy the little things, for one day you may look back and realize they were the big things."
> **—Robert Brault**

YES, THERE ARE PROBLEMS

Enjoyment can come from playing, working, or having fun. It can come being in a moment of calm, appreciating progress, listening to your favorite music or even the smell of coffee in the morning. Enjoyment has many sources, but it can only be found and experienced today.

That said, problems can also be found today, and they can bring anxiety, stress, and worry, preventing you from enjoying your possibilities. Do any of these sound familiar?

- ➢ Getting anxious about what might happen pulls your attention away from the good in today.
- ➢ Dwelling on regret, guilt, or disappointment makes today feel smaller or less meaningful.
- ➢ Getting trapped in analysis, doubt, or "what-ifs" makes it hard to be present.

Enjoy Today

- Feeling "behind" or like you're "not enough" based on others' lives steals your daily joy.
- Succumbing to internal criticism shapes the day as something to survive, not enjoy.
- Allowing stress, sadness, or unprocessed emotions to reign quietly robs you of your enjoyment.
- Doing the same thing every day without renewal dulls your senses.
- Suffering from long-term stress narrows your perspective, hiding small joys from view.
- Overlooking everyday successes flattens the emotional highs of life.
- Experiencing pain, illness, or mental health challenges overshadows lighter moments.
- Being constantly exposed to problems and bad news shapes a darker worldview.
- Taking time for granted makes it easier to miss the value in today.
- Feeling loneliness and separation darkens the beauty of the day.

"Life isn't easy—get used to it."
—Bill Gates

Yes, There Are Problems

Problems come and go, sometimes one at a time and sometimes in clusters. They range from frustrating and sad to overwhelming and painful, presenting a tangible challenge that requires a solution. How you see them and how long they last play a big role in how they affect you and you affect them. The specifics of these problems include (but are certainly not limited to) the following:

Surface-level problems: These are easily identifiable and often temporary or situational. They can last for days and weeks and usually have straightforward solutions.

Examples: Time management issues, minor conflicts with friends or colleagues, simple bad habits, or avoiding exercise.

Mid-level problems: These require more introspection to understand fully and are often persistent but not debilitating. They can last for weeks and months and may need a sustained effort to address.

Examples: Career dissatisfaction, relationship issues, moderate anxiety, financial issues, seeing everyday events as worrying, and not being able to look on the "bright" side.

Deep-rooted problems: They may be partially or fully subconscious and often stem from past experiences or trauma. They can last for months and years and usually require professional help and/or significant personal work.

Examples: Chronic depression, financial issues, severe self-esteem issues, addiction.

Life-challenging problems: These can be personal and/or affect family and friends. They usually require professional support, care, and time as an elixir.

Examples: Debilitating sickness, family tragedy, incurable disease.

There's a lot of shit out there.

The first step in overcoming a problem is recognizing its magnitude, nature, and root cause. This awareness gives you a foundation for finding solutions and reclaiming your ability to move forward.

Worries, on the other hand, are the anticipation of a negative outcome, whether or not it actually happens. They, too, create stress and test your resilience, adaptability, and inner strength. In addition to the worries created by the problems mentioned are the worries that reside in thoughts and emotions. These worries are less obvious, and this type of worry, in itself, becomes a problem.

Call them "true-self problems," which are deeply individual yet surprisingly universal. They can repeat on a never-ending loop and linger as stress, influencing your decisions, lifestyle, and interactions with the world. Some examples include how you see the world or think the world sees you, low self-esteem, focusing on what's missing instead of what's there, beating yourself up, and being unable to change.

The truth is that older generations were not taught how to deal with these problems, and new generations, while trying to raise

Yes, There Are Problems

their kids to be more enlightened, are facing new and evolving problems.

Though true-self problems are part of the human experience, exposing some of their root causes can, for some, lead to clarity and a helpful awareness. Here, you'll find thoughts on what a few of these root causes might be. I call them "voices."

> Ours is such a short moment on this earth.
> Don't let the good bits pass you by.

ARE "GROWING UP VOICES" CHALLENGING YOU?

Past clings like a vine,
Roots dig deep, choke present growth,
Struggle to break free.

What does it mean to be truly yourself? The true self is the most authentic, unfiltered version of you—free from the weight of societal expectations, fears, and the roles you are obligated to play. It's easy to say but much harder to do.

Let's face it: life has a way of burying this true self under layers of responsibility, comparison, and the constant pressure to meet others' expectations.

These can come from "growing-up voices" that aren't clear-cut problems, such as loss or health concerns, and many people don't see them as problems. Their presence is "just the way it is," and they become the quiet undercurrents that run beneath and shape your daily life.

These voices grew as you were learning to be "yourself." They are not problems in themselves, but whether quiet or loud, optimistic or pessimistic, they influenced you with the needs and views of others that may still affect you today.

It's like wearing glasses you've forgotten you're wearing—they color everything you see, yet you rarely stop to examine the lenses themselves.

Imagine feeling stuck in a way you can't quite explain—like something essential is missing. Maybe you're overwhelmed by cycles of worry, the pull to complain, comparisons that steal your joy, or anxiety over things you can't control.

It's not just "life being hard." It's about how your perspective might work against you instead of for you. Sometimes, it's simply forgetting the ways of thinking and feeling that support you enjoying more.

Over time, this disconnect from your true self can leave you feeling out of place, unsure of your next steps, or vaguely uneasy, even when things seem "fine." They each have a familiar ring:

- ➢ **As a child**, you depended on your parents and teachers to guide you; their ideas shaped your own.
- ➢ **As a teenager**, you sought acceptance, so the approval and comments of friends became a significant influence.

Are "Growing Up Voices" Challenging You?

> **As a young adult**, you faced unique challenges and stresses, navigating a transitional period that included careers, children, lifestyles, and self-discovery.

These influences create a mixed tapestry of beliefs that often work below your conscious awareness. If they reinforce your *true self*, great; if not, the whispers of *"Why me?"* or *"What else?"* creep in. It's as if you're seeing the world through a filter you don't even notice or there's a background melody playing in your mind that you no longer consciously listen to.

> Do you recognize these "growing-up voices" in your life?

> When you doubt yourself, whose voice does it sound like?

> Is there something you disliked growing up that you still do today?

> What advice would you give yourself to enjoy more of today?

Their voices still speak,
but as I watch from a calm distance,
mine becomes more clear.

ARE THE VOICES OF OTHERS AFFECTING YOU?

Many voices hum;
you pick one and call it truth.
Was it ever yours?

Your "growing-up voices" can influence you in good and bad ways. So, you play the hand you're dealt, right? Well, yes, but new cards are always being dealt by intelligent, talented, always-on voices who are very good at commanding your attention. These voices are not concerned about appreciating your uniqueness and helping you enjoy yourself. They make you forget to pause, ask yourself what you truly enjoy, and listen to your answers.

> ➢ **Advertisers, marketers, and those selling** tell you what to do, what will work, and what's best. They offer results that are better than ever—the big promises. Some

may provide direction or inspiration, but *these messages are created to grab your attention—and your money.*

- ➢ **News and Media Companies** repeatedly try to scare you with what's wrong, terrible, or negative! They share stories of dramatic loss, crisis, and disaster, showing extremes of anxiety and worry. *Of course, they want your eyeballs—and your money, too.*

- ➢ **Social Media** gives us ways of connecting and is now stirring up envy and outrage about all sorts of things using analytics and algorithms of every kind. *They, too, are very interested in your eyeballs—and, of course, your money.*

- ➢ **Work or Career** is how you make a living and rightly focuses on the work, not you. Separating personal life from work is difficult. *Because work wants your eyeballs—and will pay you for them.*

Enjoy Today is ultimately about learning to recognize these external influences and sort through the "noise" toward choices that align with your truths. It's not ignoring the world around you; it's about developing a resilient internal guide that promises more satisfaction and enjoyment in life.

- ➢ Do you recognize these "voices of others" in your life?
- ➢ Are there ones that hold you back?
- ➢ How do you deal with them?
- ➢ How would you advise yourself to deal with them?

Are The Voices Of Others Affecting You?

➤ How do you advise others to deal with them?

> A thousand eyes blink;
> you mirror without knowing.
> Which face is your own?

YES, THERE ARE PRACTICES TO ENJOY MORE

"The limits to the possibilities in your life tomorrow are the buts you use today."
—**Les Brown**

Possibilities are infinite.

Practice makes them specific.

Enjoy Today offers practices for picking and supporting your own directions. They increase focus on the possibilities of today, help clarify paths, guide you to focus on your strengths, and be grateful for what you have and have been given. I believe that, collectively, they are instrumental in guiding you to Enjoy Today.

These practices do not involve fixing every problem or controlling every aspect of your life. They are about ways of building a mindset that helps you to take the steps you desire, even in the face of uncertainty.

The key lies not in rigid instructions or following a formula but in universal principles—because no single solution works for everyone.

Here, you'll find flexible guidelines designed to meet you where you are. Their purpose is simple: to spark reflection, encourage growth, and inspire meaningful action that feels true to you. Use them if you like.

Your life, your practice, and your possibilities will be uniquely yours.

Only you can determine what that means for you.

Trust yourself to adapt and apply these practices to fit who you are.

Practicing will increase your possibilities and offer many benefits.

I've found that possibilities also present themselves and then go away, though some do linger. I've been with my wife, Patty, for over fifty years. That possibility was certainly one that "lingered" for me. It took a series of coincidences for us to begin dating and then continued coincidences for us to continue dating. It was only then that the longer-term possibilities presented themselves. But that is a story for another time.

Yes, There Are Practices To Enjoy More

Choice, a whispered path.
One step sets the journey's course.
Destiny unfolds.

1. A PTR PRACTICE: REFRESHES YOUR MOMENTS

"The music is not in the notes,
but in the silence between."
—Wolfgang Amadeus Mozart

Let's break a rule or perhaps create a new one: Don't push through when you hit a wall and need to go further. Stop. Pause. These moments aren't signs of weakness; they're transitions. They are times when your strengths are calling for renewal, asking you to regroup and reclaim your energy. You're not stalling; you're gearing up for better, more robust next *small steps*.

That's right—stop the hurry and embrace the pause. Instead of forcing your way through, let the moment become a tool for clarity, strength, and renewal. When you hear yourself saying, *"I can't do it."* or *"I need to rest,"* those aren't just complaints—

they're signals. Signals that it's time to listen to your inner voice and reset.

A nap can be refreshing when it's a busy day and you get tired, you didn't sleep well the night before, or you simply want to relax and get a new perspective. Naps seem to be especially useful during that afternoon dip—usually between 1 p.m. and 4 p.m.—when your circadian rhythms naturally slow you down. Naps are the resets that help restore your energy.

Whether you call them naps, quick rests, or simply a moment to catch your breath, naps are pauses and your body's way of reminding you to slow down to keep moving forward. Your body is saying, *"I need a break; let me recharge."*

When the calendar is full or everything seems to be rushed, it feels like a privilege to take a nap. That said, I'd like to share a practice called PTR (Pause To REfresh). It's a deliberate pause and can be used anytime and anywhere to recharge and renew your abilities—with more focus. It's more than a nap; it's an intentional way to address mental, emotional, and creative needs. It can be done anywhere, anytime—as quietly and quickly as you desire—or as long and as deeply as you need.

Naps recharge your body.

PTR is a refresh button for your thinking—with purpose.

THE POWER OF "RE" WORDS

Enter the power of "RE" words to purposely rethink priorities, release stress, refocus directions, or rejuvenate during the day.

Yes, There Are Practices To Enjoy More

The prefix "RE" typically means "again" or "back" and is used to indicate repetition or a return to a previous state. To REframe is to see something from a different perspective. To REnew is to create something new. To REconsider or REthink is to think about something again, often with a fresh perspective.

You know Rewords—words like rest, reimagine, restore and recharge. These aren't just words; they're tools to shift your mindset. They allow you to stop, breathe, take another look at your progress, and see what's right in front of you. Have you ever intentionally used REwords to improve your day?

REwords empower so many things, including transitions, perspectives, relationships, abilities, jobs, and roles. These REwords have many cousins and they all offer an opportunity to ground yourself in the present. They encourage mindfulness and help you appreciate where you are rather than being stuck where you think you should be.

By intentionally embracing REwords and PTR, you give yourself the grace to slow down, be creative, see the challenge differently, and unlock another way forward. Instead of pushing harder, you allow yourself to reimagine or recommit to your approach.

- ➢ REwords help your thinking become more flexible.
- ➢ REwords guide and improve clarity.
- ➢ REwords build little mental bridges to new ideas or feelings.
- ➢ REwords generate paths forward.

- REwords bring you renewed energy and focus.
- REwords offer the benefits of unplugging and REplugging.

> A purposeful pause for RE-thinking.
> A reset for RE-silience.
> A RE-imagining during times of transition.

WHY YOU SHOULD GIVE IT A TRY

PTR (Pause To REfresh) is your practice for using REwords. It's accessible at any time and always flexible to your needs. Embracing the power to RE-anything allows you to recognize opportunities, seize moments more fully, and perhaps see another path that may be right in front of you.

Use this practice when navigating a creative block, recovering from a stressful moment, or seeking a moment of calm. Whether you pause for a minute or linger longer, it's all about what suits your needs. Even a few moments of truly listening to yourself can bring surprising clarity, calm, and insight.

In the fields of neuroscience, psychology, and psychiatry, the brain's awareness of internal states and how you listen to yourself from the inside out is called *interoception*. It improves when we pause and "listen" to ourselves. This self-awareness activates the *insula* and *prefrontal cortex* areas, which are linked to emotional regulation, decision-making, and clarity.

Yes, There Are Practices To Enjoy More

Interoception is related to a "gut feeling," but it's broader and more nuanced. A gut feeling is a fast, intuitive sense that something is right or wrong—often emotionally charged and felt in the body (especially the stomach). It's your body's way of giving you rapid feedback based on past experiences, emotions, and unconscious processing. A gut feeling is the message.

Interoception is the underlying mechanism that allows you to notice that gut feeling in the first place. It's your brain's ability to sense and interpret signals from inside the body—not just the gut, but also heart rate, muscle tension, breath, and more, enabling you to receive and understand it.

PTR is a practice that will help you listen, adapt, and fit whatever you're hearing into your day. Do you need to restore depleted energy? Would you like to reset your mind and body? Would seeing things differently add clarity or creativity? Is there something you're stressing about or perhaps overthinking?

HOW TO PRACTICE PTR

The first step in visualizing the "RE" you need is to create a quiet moment and take the time to hear yourself speak. To physically get ready, give yourself a small buffer from the pressures of the moment.

> - **Find a quiet spot**. Choose the quietest place available.
> - **Get comfortable**. Sit or lie down in a position that feels good.

Enjoy Today

- **Breathe consciously.** Take slow inhales and exhales to calm your body and mind, and continue as needed throughout your practice.

- **Begin repeating your time-based mantra***
  - **Check the time** on a clock.
  - **Create your mantra** based on the current time.
    - If it's 2:34, your mantra becomes "2-3-4."
    - If it's 4:16, your mantra becomes "4-1-6."
    - If it's 11:23, your mantra becomes "1-1-2-3."

- **Close your eyes.** To minimize distractions and allow yourself to focus on your inner thoughts and needs.

- **Keep breathing and begin to repeat this time-based mantra** to yourself. Continue as needed to stay focused during your pause.

*Classically, a mantra is a repeated word, phrase, or sound used to focus the mind during meditation. The benefits include quieting mental distractions, promoting calm, and increasing clarity. This **time-based mantra** is much the same. It's a quick mental shift that centers you, bringing your attention away from the rush or fatigue of the day and back to what you desire to bring into your day.

The second step is to begin listening to yourself more consciously, to hear what you're thinking and feeling.

Yes, There Are Practices To Enjoy More

- **Let what you're listening to guide you.**

    Thoughts will come and go, and you can let them pass (like a cloud in the sky) or ask yourself why they're there for you.

    Listen to that thought, let it go, or ask yourself if there's another way you can think about it.

    Are there possible new directions you imagine might work for you?

    Listen to those thoughts, let them go, or dig deeper into why they came up and where they might be guiding you.

    Are there possible new directions you imagine might work for you?

    Listen and develop, or just let the thought pass and go on to the next cloud.

    Repeat.

The third step, having relaxed with breath and mantra and listened to where you're guiding yourself, is to focus on the specific "RE" that fits what you want from your thinking.

- **Visualize your RE.** Allow yourself to visualize what you need. For example:
    - If you're trying to **REst**, picture yourself relaxing in a peaceful setting.
    - If you're trying to **REthink**, imagine different solutions or perspectives coming to you.

Enjoy Today

- o If you're in need of **REenergizing**, see yourself moving quickly and easily.

> - **This practice naturally evolves.** You begin with focusing on the breath, your mantra, listening, and your specific REs, and you may transition into a meditative state. Some even report that their TFM (TOSSLY Flow Meditation) emerges during PTR, as they combine this technique with a deeper reflection.

> - **End when ready.** When you've completed your PTR, your eyes will open (and if you're using a time-based mantra, you can recheck the time and see how long you were engaged). If you have a limited window, set a timer; you will still find benefits, and you can return to PTR when you have more time.

> My PTRs naturally last around twenty minutes, though, depending on the events of the day, sometimes I open my eyes sooner. They may even last longer when many thoughts and ideas are being presented.

PTR, like all practices, takes repetition to gain proficiency. It might take you ten days, or it could take you thirty. Here's my recommendation: Start. Do PTR in the moments you recognize might call for it. By practicing this way just a few times, I expect you'll start to feel the benefits. If not, see what might be getting in the way and adjust accordingly.

To Enjoy Today is about intentionally seeing and changing your moments in your favor, and PTR is a foundational way to do so.

Yes, There Are Practices To Enjoy More

"Almost everything will work again if you unplug it for a few minutes, including you."
—**Anne Lamott**

2. A BIT PRACTICE: SHIFTS YOUR MINDSET TO ENJOY TODAY.

"You are alive today, and that's enough reason to celebrate and make the most of it."
—**Orison Swett Marden**

The word "best" describes the highest degree of quality, excellence, or desirability and can provide powerful motivations and goals in performance, choices, qualities, or achievements. By expanding this definition of "best" to focus on today and the benefits it brings, you extract more enjoyment and meaning from each day.

Choosing to see the best in today, this one day, is a small step forward toward Enjoy Today. It's not about ignoring hardships or pretending to be happy; rather, it's about guiding your mind to notice, appreciate, and savor the good things, big and small, in today's events and perspectives. To find the extraordinary in the ordinary and make every day count in its unique way.

Supporting this opportunity is a BIT (See The Best In Today) practice. You use it to notice and build upon the good things in your day that may otherwise have gone unnoticed. In just a few intentional moments, you think about your day's best moments and write them down.

> "Don't count the days; make the days count."
> **—Muhammad Ali**

WHY YOU SHOULD GIVE IT A TRY

There will be days when problems like illness, sadness, or something you've loved or worked hard for is lost or doesn't materialize. Problems and the worries that come with them will fill your mind.

I remember the moment when I stepped off a curb in New York City and my knee shot pain through my body, leading to years of doctor recommendations. Then, of course, there were the financial pressures that popped up, the health scares, the deaths of people we loved, and even the vicious colds and flus that caught up with us. And when Patty and I wanted to have children, we couldn't; it took five years for that "problem" to resolve. I could go on, but does any of that sound familiar to you?

Using BIT to look for the best moments of your day gives you a response to these problems, these "bad" feelings, and is part of honoring the effort, energy, and hope you invested. Sadness, then, isn't bad; it's a necessary release and a way to process disappointment and find the strength to move forward. *If recognizing sadness is the best you can offer today, recognize that each day is unique and that appreciating what it offers will bring opportunities, even on difficult days—maybe especially on difficult days.*

Is a BIT practice for you? After all, you're busy, used to dealing with problems, waiting for big moments, reminiscing about "the good old days," or perhaps not seeing the benefits of struggle. And when things go wrong, you rightfully worry.

Well, here's the thing: You don't need to wait for everything to get better or for special occasions or accomplishments. You can see what's best about today if you choose to see it that way. By taking a few minutes to reflect, you can guide yourself to what you appreciate today.

BIT encourages you to fully embrace the present, find the extraordinary in the ordinary, and make every day count in its unique way. At first, it may be challenging to see the "best," but that's okay. Over time, you'll start to notice things you previously overlooked.

HOW TO START A BIT PRACTICE

All you need to begin is a blank notebook or pad dedicated to seeing the best in today (paper is preferred over digital). Grab a pen, pencil, or even colored markers if you like, and find a handy place to keep them, like your desk, nightstand, or kitchen drawer.

Enjoy Today

- Open a fresh page. At the top, write one of the phrases below. You can use all of them or focus on one. Box the phrase for emphasis. This will be your daily affirmation and reminder. The mere act of writing it down and boxing it will focus you on finding it.

    a. **"Today Is the Best Day of My Life . . ."** Note underneath it anything big or small that makes you smile, appreciate what you have, or simply recognize the possibilities of being alive. I've used this over the years and found so many things to appreciate about my day.

    b. **"I See the Best in Today Because . . ."** Again, write underneath that phrase things, big or small, that made you smile, show your progress, or that you're grateful for having (or will have in the future) in your life.

    c. **"My Person of the Day Is . . ."** Select a special person you've come across during your day. Someone who offered a kind smile, comment, or perhaps generous support in a time of need. A friendly salesperson? Someone you chatted with on a walk? Someone who understood you? Patty uses this consistently to recognize a person who brightened her day.

- Pausing after you've written your affirmation allows the good things—the "best" things in your day—to surface. Some examples would be:

d. Considering the ideas, pets, or people that made you smile.

   e. Paying attention to the sensory experiences that bring you joy, like the view outside your window, the aroma of your morning coffee, or the warmth of sunlight on your face.

   f. Thinking about moments where your body or mind helped you in walking, breathing, or thinking clearly.

   g. Seeing that small things, even minor achievements or positive feelings, are worth celebrating.

   h. Acknowledging that on some days, releasing sadness or loss is the "best" you can do, and that's OK.

➤ Note under your affirmation whatever comes to mind—one word, a few lines, or even a doodle. This isn't a test; it's you finding and talking to yourself about the simple things, the steps you're taking, or the people who brought you joy. In doing so daily, you begin to recognize and focus on the "best" things in your day, and you will realize you can find them every day.

➤ The next day, continue on a new page or below your previous entry by writing your affirmation ("Today Is the Best Day of My Life," "I See the Best in Today Because . . . ," or "My Person of the Day Is . . .") and again box it for emphasis. Pause, consider, and note the moments or people that brought joy, made you smile, or helped you feel capable and resilient.

Enjoy Today

- Then, going forward, take a few minutes every day, the good days and the bad days, to write what you enjoyed about your day.

- Daily repetition, especially for the first thirty days, is needed to establish BIT as a habit. With repetition, you'll begin to see and appreciate more of the good things in your day that you may have been overlooking.

- While there are many ways to establish a habit, James Clear, in his book *Atomic Habits*, introduces the concept of habit stacking: "One of the best ways to build a new habit is to identify a current habit you already do each day and then stack your new behavior on top."

- Expecting resistance is perfectly natural; at first, you might think, *"How can this be my best day?"* or *"Who was the nicest person I met today?"* Thinking about it is key, and if your answer is a simple word or phrase or just that you're alive today, that's OK.

- Consistency is vital, but flexibility is fine—if life gets busy, don't feel pressured. The goal is progress, not perfection. If you miss a few days, don't worry. Pick it up the next day and continue.

- After a while, your mind will naturally begin to see more of the "best" around you. Writing BIT daily may be unnecessary, but it will always be available to use.

- Look back at your daily entries, say once a month, and you'll notice how many positive moments you experienced. This reflection will make you more aware of the good things in each day, and that will, in turn, make you more aware of what you truly enjoy in your life.

TIPS FOR SUCCESS

1. **Be Consistent:** Life can be hectic, and you might miss a few days. Simply pick up where you left off without any pressure.

2. **Stay Present:** Focus on the small things that make today special. There's no need to wait for significant achievements or milestones.

3. **Celebrate Variety:** Every day is different. Some might be full of success, others simple pleasures, and still others sadness—embrace them all.

Ready to give it a try?

It's free, simple, and can be done anytime or anywhere.

Open a page, write down your affirmation, and begin.

> "Today is life—the only life you are sure of.
> Make the most of today."
> **—Dale Carnegie**

3. A TFM PRACTICE: GUIDES YOU THROUGHOUT YOUR DAY

What you need—When you need it.
Requesting Support.
Recognizing Accomplishment.
Being Grateful.

Many years ago, I learned a Transcendental Meditation (TM) practice. I went to a class, received a mantra (I was told it was personal, private, and not to be shared), and was directed to practice for twenty minutes in the morning and twenty minutes in the late afternoon. I practiced for many years and still appreciate its benefits, including reduced stress and anxiety as well as improved focus and clarity.

Over the last few years, I've also learned another "meditation" that's excellent for supporting moments and enjoying today. That meditation, which I call TOSSLY Flow Meditation (TFM), is a versatile, self-guided practice designed to help direct and support internal thoughts and feelings as they surface throughout the day. You can call on it intentionally or practice anytime during the moments of your day that call for it.

WHY YOU SHOULD GIVE IT A TRY

We all have an internal narrative, our self-talk, that's always on and always talking with us. In creating TFM meditations, you are developing and giving yourself responses to *guide, affirm,* and *appreciate* yourself. It seems obvious once you begin: It's a good thing to have a simple, flexible way to shape the narratives you desire.

TFM is built around practices that we call *In.sights*. They can be used together or separately, as needed, for focusing your intentions, recognizing your strengths, and expressing gratitude. Calling on them gives you a way to feel calmer, clearer, and stronger. You just have to be willing to pause, even for a breath. Like a moving meditation, there is no need to close your eyes, though you can if you like.

HOW TO CREATE IN.SIGHTS

In.sights come from you, listening to yourself, and choosing what you desire to bring into your life, what you see yourself actually accomplishing, and what you are thankful for.

I recommend writing them using a digital app like Notes to keep them easily accessible for use, review, addition, modification, or deletion as needed. This adaptable approach keeps your In.sights personal, relevant, and in tune with your daily needs.

You'll find an evolving quality in TFM, which is a natural reflection of personal growth. Some In.sights will naturally be added, overlap, shift categories, and be removed as your life changes. These shifts are natural, allowing you to see and celebrate your progress and momentum. Over time, In.sights that once felt aspirational can become statements of accomplishment, moving to "thank you" as they integrate into your daily life.

Remember, effective In.sights are authentic and meaningful to you. They are personal guided meditations and tools created by you, for you to use. As you repeat them, expect the words and feelings to adjust and clarify to be even more naturally personal.

You create In.sights from frameworks in three areas. As you read the examples below, consider how you would make their phrasing personal to you. That said, here's a guide to effectively creating and using them.

1. "May I . . ." In.sights*

With "May I . . . ," you set, support, and guide your personal desires, directions, and intentions. You make requests of yourself, or the universe, that can be called on at any time.

Steps to create a "May I . . ." In.sight:
1. Think about what you want to achieve or experience in your life.

2. Write it in a concise and specific statement, starting with "May I . . ."
3. Keep it positive.

Examples:

- ➢ May I be happy and positive.
- ➢ May I have energy and stay motivated.
- ➢ May I work hard and contribute.
- ➢ May I be well and healthy.
- ➢ May I love and be loved.

If "May I . . ." is not the way you personally would ask for this support, consider starting with "Please support me . . . ," "I pray . . . ," or "I open myself to . . ."

2. "I Am . . ." In.sights

With "I am . . ." you recognize what you are accomplishing, affirm positive qualities, and acknowledge what is going right.

Steps to create an "I Am . . ." In.sight:

1. Notice when you are happy with your life and progress.
2. Notice the positive attributes and achievements in your life.
3. Write them down concisely, starting with "I Am . . ."
4. Always use present tense and positive language.

Examples:

- ➢ I am accomplishing my goal (be specific).
- ➢ I am hardworking and able.
- ➢ I am kind and generous.
- ➢ I am loved and do love.
- ➢ I am peacefully at ease.

3. "Thank you . . ." In.sights*

With "Thank you . . ." you express, acknowledge, and recognize what you have in life. What you've been given, achieved, and those who've supported you. "Thank you . . ." In.sights could also start with "I'm grateful for . . ." or "I appreciate . . ."

Steps to create a "Thank You . . ." In.sight:

1. Recognize what you are grateful for.
2. Be specific about what you're thankful for.
3. Write it down concisely, starting with "Thank you . . ."
4. These expressions should make you smile at your good fortune.

Examples:

- ➢ Thank you for my progress.
- ➢ Thank you for my health and well-being.

Enjoy Today

- Thank you to my family.
- Thank you for the love in my life.
- Thank you for the small joys of each day.

*Some have wondered, "Who are you addressing when you say 'May I . . .' or 'Thank you . . .'? Is it God?" It could be, but it doesn't have to be. TFM is more about recognizing the combinations of people, ideas, and experiences that enrich one's life.

WHEN TO USE TFM

TFM can be used in a variety of ways and at several different times, including:

- **As a Morning Ritual:** Start your day by reviewing your In.sights to set a positive tone and intention for the day ahead.

- **Throughout the Day**: Allow your In.sights to surface naturally during daily activities to support you. For example, when thinking of a goal or intention: *"May I . . . (fill in the intention)."* When thinking about how you have accomplished something: *"I Am . . . (fill in what you're doing)."* When experiencing moments of appreciation: *"Thank you . . . (for what you appreciate)."*

- **As an Evening Reflection**: End your day by revisiting your In.sights. Reflect on how they manifested throughout your day and consider if any need adjusting.

- **In Mindful Moments**: Use the appropriate In.sights during brief pauses in your day—while waiting in line, during a coffee break, or before a get-together.

- **At Stressful Moments:** If the pressures of the day are building, calling on the appropriate In.sights can offer relief.

- **Combined with Other Practices**: Your In.sights may pop up automatically in your other mindfulness or meditation practices.

TIPS FOR CREATING EFFECTIVE IN.SIGHTS:

1. **Write them:** In a notebook or phone app like Notes, write them so you can see them, and keep them readily available to review and update.

2. **Review them daily or periodically:** Reviewing keeps them fresh and easy to recall.

3. **Make them personal:** Phrase them as statements, not questions, that should resonate with your life experiences and aspirations.

4. **Keep them positive:** Frame your In.sights positively, focusing on what you want and have rather than what you don't want.

5. **Be specific:** The more specific your In.sights, the more powerful and meaningful they'll be.

6. **Review and revise:** As your life and days change, delete, modify, or create new In.sights to keep them relevant and impactful.

7. **Start small:** There is no right or wrong amount. Begin with just a few in each category and gradually add more as you become comfortable with the practice.

YOUR 20-DAY TFM CHALLENGE

Honestly, there is no secret in having a twenty-day timeframe. I picked the number randomly, and everybody likes a challenge, right?

Certainly, it takes repetition to learn and become comfortable with anything, including TFM. Its benefits may come all at once or take a little longer to appear. As you progress, reflect on your experience and any changes you notice in your mindset or daily life. Remember, if you miss a few days, get back to it. The goal is progress, not perfection.

Ready to give it a try? Here is a day-by-day practice you can follow to establish a foundation and provide opportunities for expansion, refinement, and integration into your life.

- Days 1–5: Practice pausing and listening to yourself.
- Days 6–9: Create a few personal In.sights for "May I," "I Am," and "Thank you."
- Days 9–10: Notice the moments and places where your In.sights pop up.

- Days 11–15: Start integrating In.sights into your daily activities.
- Days 16–20: Focus on spontaneously using In.sights throughout your day.

What would you like to bring into your life?

What personal accomplishments and moments of success make you smile?

What are you grateful for?

How would you phrase your In.sights?

> Use a meditation that becomes part of you,
> as you become more of who you choose to be.

4. A W4G PRACTICE: BECOMES YOUR FRIENDLY COLLABORATOR

"Don't curse the darkness; light a candle."
—Chinese Proverb

I begin with a tip of the hat to the wonderful writers who have brought the power of writing into my life. Just a few of them include Stephen King, Julia Cameron, Anne Lamott, Eckhart Tolle, and Steven Pressfield. Their skills and teachings have brought to me, and millions of other people, an ability to see more and go further.

With those shoulders to stand on, my writing has focused on how people can use their moments to Enjoy Today. It's not really about writing well; it's about a bridge between your thoughts and your actions. I call it Writing 4 Growth, or W4G. I believe it to be a transformative way to bring order and understanding to your thoughts, clarify your perspectives, and guide your small steps in the directions you choose.

W4G is not a way for you to write better—rather, it's a way to put the power of writing into your hands.

- ➢ It's not about how you write; it's about how you use writing to connect with yourself.

- ➢ It does not require grammar, punctuation, or technical skills; it's private, with no grading or review by others.

- ➢ It's free and can be done anytime, anywhere, in any format that feels right for you.

- ➢ It's meant to be, and to become, a friendly collaboration with yourself to harness your strengths and illuminate the possibilities ahead.

You can write about anything that comes to mind: what happened during your day, what's bothering you, or what you're excited about. You can even simply offer yourself advice. Whatever it is, you benefit from seeing the additional personal perspective that writing provides.

W4G literally gives you another
perspective on what you're thinking.

WHY YOU SHOULD GIVE IT A TRY

If you have already incorporated writing into your life, you know it's a powerful practice that helps you get out of your head and increase your self-awareness.

Perhaps writing has never appealed to you. Maybe past attempts at journaling helped you "get it out" but didn't seem to take you anywhere. Or, like many, you might feel hesitant, comparing yourself to others, and only want to write "well." Well, it's important to remember that no one sees this personal writing except you, and there are plenty of benefits waiting for you.

Are you ready to light the candle that writing provides? Here are proven principles and straightforward practices designed to show you how to use writing to take small, intentional steps toward more fully enjoying life today.

> "The mind is not a vessel to be filled,
> but a fire to be kindled."
> **—Plutarch**

HOW TO START A W4G PRACTICE

GIVE YOURSELF A SPACE TO EXPRESS YOURSELF

Thinking is nonsense,
and writing makes sense of it.

A first step with W4G is getting your thoughts out where you can see them. Whether on paper or digitally, daily or periodically, this step allows your thoughts and feelings to unfold and become more apparent. Writing about these thoughts and feelings—an act many call journaling—is the beginning of seeing more clearly what you're saying to yourself.

Write in any way that suits you because there's no right or wrong. However you do it, you will gain insights about your true self. You might begin with simple doodling, one-line observations, or asking yourself questions and answering them.

The more you write, the easier it becomes. As you grow more comfortable, you may or may not write more extended reflections or even fill entire pages. You might be surprised by what surfaces.

> Think of W4G as a conversation with
> yourself on paper.

If you already journal, you know how to do this. And if you haven't, all it takes to begin is a blank page and a few minutes to see what comes up. Here's a brief exercise to help you get started:

1. Grab a piece of paper (or open a new document on your device).
2. Set a timer for just a few minutes (or more if you like).
3. Write or doodle whatever comes to mind—don't worry about grammar, punctuation, or structure.
4. If you're unsure where to start, try writing about one of these topics:
   - Something you're grateful for.
   - How you felt when you woke up.
   - A moment from your day that stood out.
   - A worry that's been circling in your mind.
5. Just let the words (or doodles) flow.
6. When the timer goes off, take a moment to read what you've written.
7. What you see is another perspective of what's in your head.

8. You can literally adjust, add to, or delete this perspective if you choose.

Did you notice how it helped you express and focus your thoughts? Did it increase awareness? Did it give you another perspective on your feelings?

Do it again the next day and see what comes out. I recommend having a pad of paper and your writing instruments nearby wherever you sit on a regular basis to make doodling and jotting down notes easier.

Over time, you'll see the benefits of having another perspective, including increased clarity, a better ability to focus, and a way to guide your choices and decisions to do the following:

- Add visibility to your inner world to better understand and navigate it.
- Capture your excitement and motivation.
- Celebrate and repeat what works.
- Surface your worries and doubts to make them more understandable.
- Clarify your thinking to see what might be holding you back.
- Bring sharper focus to your life and the actions needed to move forward.
- Make repetition, modification, and improved memory more accessible.

Enjoy Today

> ➤ Reinforce lessons and insights to help them stick and grow.

It's worth repeating: There's no right way to do W4G, only your way. You're the writer, reader, and audience all at once. Use writing whenever inspiration or worry strikes to capture a fleeting thought or process your deeper feelings.

To gain the benefits of repetition, challenge yourself to see your true self again for the next seven days. Then, daily or periodically, whenever thoughts swirl, you can uncover more, and the more you do it, the more benefits will come.

> Listening to others is important;
> listening to yourself is enlightening.

PICK—AND FOLLOW— YOUR OWN DIRECTIONS

"You have brains in your head. You have feet in your shoes. You can steer yourself in any direction you choose."
—Dr. Seuss

While giving yourself a space to express yourself yields insights, clarity, and direction, picking and following your own directions nurtures your growth and keeps you moving forward. You could move toward a goal (like exercising more), embrace a purpose (like being a better friend), live a value (like showing kindness), or pursue a direction (like learning something new).

Recognizing what you want and guiding yourself toward it are both important steps. The guiding, the getting to it, is done in a transitional space where progress is unfolding but not yet complete. You need to keep yourself on track because growth is generally not easy, and it doesn't happen all at once. Instead, it occurs with *small steps* and the intentional repetition you make in cultivating your progress.

This guiding step is a journey, not a final destination. As Ursula K. Le Guin wisely said, *"It is good to have an end to journey toward, but it is the journey that matters, in the end."*

The practices of Enjoy Today will pave the way. There are also classic techniques for guiding yourself, each with a proven track record of success across various situations. You can use these techniques separately or in combination.

Each is a storytelling approach that uses the power of positive self-talk—with you as the main character. These techniques shape your script. Storytelling is a timeless method used to engage emotions, and with consistent repetition, you will cultivate belief in the story you tell yourself.

> "Logic will get you from A to B.
> Imagination will take you everywhere."
> **—Albert Einstein**

1. **Visualization**: *"To see it is to believe it."* Imagining pictures of what you want as already accomplished helps you mentally map out the steps to get there, sparking ideas and reinforcing beliefs in your ability to achieve it. For example, if you want to see your upper body stronger and more defined see yourself easily doing push ups.

2. **Affirmations**: *"Your mind believes what you tell it."* Repeating present-tense, positive statements as though

they've already happened helps make them happen. For example, "I do five push-ups daily and feel better than ever." First-person affirmations emphasize the joy of accomplishment and encourage your mind to believe in the reality of what you're saying.

3. **Intentions**: *"I intend to do five push-ups a day."* While affirmations declare something is already achieved, intentions focus on what you will do, setting your sights on the path ahead rather than the final destination. Telling yourself positively and confidently what you plan to do creates a vivid target, and repeating it to yourself reinforces your message and sharpens your aim. For example, "I intend to do five push-ups a day." "I intend to do five push-ups a day." "I intend to do five push-ups a day."

4. **Prayer**: *"May I find the strength to do five push-ups a day."* When you're stuck, uncertain, or facing unknowns along your path, prayer serves as a request for guidance or strength from a Higher Power.

5. **Use a 2-Be List**: *"Focus on what you want 2-Become."* To build a 2-Be list, start by noticing ideas and moments that make you smile and inspire and/or excite you. Note things that represent habits you'd like to build or skills you'd like to learn. Include people you've learned from, quotes that resonate with you, and ideas for your future. Capturing and keeping a 2-Be list and referring to it regularly energizes you and brings more of what you

want into your life. For example, "I do ten push-ups and ten squats every day." Have fun with it.

To gain more benefits, consider creating a single place to keep and review your visions, intentions, and lists. Then, every thirty days or so, revisit them to re-engage with the ideas that inspired you. This, too, is a *small step* that guides you in inviting more of what you want into your life.

> When you see something you admire,
> write it down—and keep it.

How you guide yourself is up to you, but it will always involve sharpening your focus on your chosen direction and filtering out distractions. With an "end in mind," you can navigate life's twists and turns to stay on track:

- Picture what you want so you can set your direction and gain clarity.

- The more emotionally you connect to it, the more "real" it becomes.

- Repetition provides practice to better guide your steps.

- If you're smiling, it's a good sign you're on the right track.

- As you move toward what scares you, it often unlocks strength and understanding.

- Progress is rarely a straight line. Knowing this enlightens your progress.

- Detours and challenges are part of growth; see them as learning opportunities.
- Positive guidance creates a supportive framework for success.
- Negative guidance can work, too, but only in the short term.
- A timeframe, like "for thirty days," gives your *small steps* a clearer target.

How do you guide yourself to more of what you want?

What has worked best for you?

What would you share with others?

> "If you know where you're going,
> every step has purpose."
> **—Zig Ziglar**

WRITE PRIVATELY TO UNLOCK YOURSELF

> "Writing privately allows you to dance naked on the page, free from the eyes of critics or well-meaning friends."
> —**Julia Cameron**

In personal writing, particularly in W4G, self-censorship can limit the expression of your thoughts and feelings. That's why Writing 4 Growth is designed to be a private experience—to free yourself from outside expectations, allow yourself to consider without limits, and lessen the influence or need for approval from others. Why? Because even those with the best intentions can make you doubt yourself or offer opinions that cloud your vision.

We've all learned to censor ourselves. That's not necessarily a bad thing; there are places, people, and events where a filter comes in handy. Yet, private writing allows you to sort things out and better understand what's important to you. It gives you the time and space to practice, refine your thoughts, develop and believe in your ideas, or discard them if they don't feel right.

Writing this way is like having a one-on-one conversation with yourself. You can create or rediscover your voice, listen to your intuition, and gain insights to figure out what truly matters.

Of course, feedback and input from others are essential and always available when needed. Consider asking questions or talking about your ideas more broadly to get input without revealing the details of what you've written.

Remember, W4G is a conversation with yourself, for yourself, and no one else. It helps you to:

- ➢ Increase your creativity without the fear of making mistakes.
- ➢ Develop your ideas without worrying about what others might think.
- ➢ Write more freely without needing to explain or justify your thoughts.
- ➢ Focus on what's meaningful to you without others second-guessing.
- ➢ Be more honest with yourself.
- ➢ Explore your ideas fluidly so you can generate more of them.

Are you aware of censoring yourself around others?

Has self-censorship limited you in sharing what you're thinking?

Would privacy allow you to ask yourself and answer more questions?

Would you speak more confidently?

>Personal vulnerability is easier when it's private.

WHY DO YOU QUESTION YOURSELF?

"I have self-doubt. I have insecurity.
I have a fear of failure."
—**Kobe Bryant**

Even the best of us face doubt, insecurity, and the fear of not getting things right. This happens in everyday life—and even in private writing. You might feel comfortable putting words on the page but still find it difficult to be completely honest with yourself.

Personally, I've found that there are several reasons for this, and for me, overcoming them involves recognizing their presence, considering why they appear, and gently moving forward.

1. Self-Censorship

Private writing is meant to be just for you, so you can feel free to write anything. But when you ask yourself, *"Should I write this?"*

or *"Is this the right thing to say?"* you may be holding yourself back.

That's your inner critic speaking, often driven by the fear of how others might perceive you. Remember, whatever you write in W4G is okay—it's for you, by you. Let your thoughts flow freely so you can explore and understand them.

> The point of writing freely is to stop holding back on your true self.

2. Expecting Overnight Results

We all get impatient sometimes. You write something you want or need—and start feeling discouraged when it doesn't happen quickly. You might think, *"This isn't working. Why am I even doing this?"* But remember, your words are seeds, and seeds don't sprout overnight. They need time and care to grow into something rewarding.

> "Great things are not done by impulse, but by a series of small things brought together."
> —**Vincent Van Gogh**

3. Not Having Time

Life can feel like a constant juggling act, making it seem like there's no time to write. But we all have the same twenty-four hours in a day. It's not about finding time; it's about making time. Some days, you'll write more and dive deep; others, you might miss writing altogether, and that's okay. Time doesn't control you—you control it.

Remember to keep a notebook or phone nearby to capture your thoughts whenever you can. Even if it's just a few lines, it still counts, and if it turns into more, that would be great. If not, no worries.

> "Time is a created thing. To say 'I don't have time' is to say 'I don't want to.'"
> **—Lao Tzu**

4. Fear of Being Wrong

We all have an inner voice that tells us to be cautious. Yet, in W4G, you don't have to justify, defend, or prove anything. No one else will see it, so whatever you write is okay. If you are hesitating out of fear of being wrong, there is no "wrong" in your Writing 4 Growth.

> "The greatest mistake you can make is continually fearing you will make one."
> **—Elbert Hubbard**

5. Not Having Anything to Say

Sometimes, it feels like you've said everything there is to say. Whether it's pages and pages or just a few words, sometimes you just run out of things to write.

Enjoy Today

But even when you feel "done," it doesn't mean you don't have more to say. Your mind is always working, even if it feels blank. If you don't know what to write, acknowledge it: *"Nothing to say today." "Feeling blah." "I'm done."* Being honest about having nothing to say can be more valuable than forcing it.

> The blank page is not empty; it's filled with the honesty of having nothing to say.

5. A PERSONAL STRENGTHS PRACTICE: FOR TAKING SMALL STEPS

You may not remember your way, but you can find it. It's there for you.

While personal strength usually focuses on the physical realm, it encompasses so much more. There is a constant interplay of the mental, physical, emotional, spiritual, and temporal. I believe that, in some magical way, the combination of these personal strengths yields and guides our "gut" and "intuition."

Whatever your path or destination, your personal strengths will be called on to move you forward. All your strengths matter. It is your strengths that will get you through a tough period, help you overcome sadness, improve your relationships, enjoy a win, or feel better more often.

Each of us has these strengths, some developed and some not, and even the slightest *small-step* adjustments can make them more useful. That said, many people have learned to treat these strengths as if they function independently, often leaning on one or two while overlooking the others or using them inconsistently. Some people naturally excel in one area, while others draw strength from another, yet they are all deeply interwoven.

A physical illness can trigger emotional distress. Emotional stress can weigh heavily on our thinking. If we feel overwhelmed, connecting with Spirit can offer a sense of comfort. Moving the body can help release tensions. All strengths can be stressed by time or by running out of time.

Give this some thought: there are possibilities to be found in using personal strengths not as isolated abilities but as a dynamic, interconnected system that is deeply interwoven into our lives.

The promise is simple: using personal strengths together in support of one another will add strength, balance, and enjoyment to your moments.

And guess what? By blending and using your strengths in this way, you'll begin to notice opportunities to apply them. These opportunities may appear at unexpected moments, or they could simply be part of your everyday routines. However they surface, they will offer you a deeper sense of connection and support.

What's the catch? There isn't one.

These personal strengths are already yours. They are aspects of your personality—and they have been all along. This isn't just a concept; it's a way of living and linking them, step by step, to take control of and shape your life to Enjoy Today.

Unconventional? Perhaps.

But it works.

Once you begin to see these personal strengths as commingled and trusted allies quietly supporting you in small, meaningful ways, you'll wonder how you ever lived without them together.

The first step in connecting your strengths is simply being aware that you can.

The idea here, and in this section, is to see the possibilities of blending these strengths, one *small step* at a time, in support of one another. Over time, by thinking about them and making slight adjustments, you will often find that they can and will come together to improve your next steps and results.

In the following sections, you'll find *small steps* to use your thinking, body, emotion, spirit, and time in support of each other. In the following list, these steps are combined; you might use some regularly, and you may never think about others.

I ask you to consider all of them, one at a time, because everything can be a source of fuel, and being able to call on a variety of personal strengths when you need them will provide benefits.

> ➢ **Being Open** – *Small steps* that embrace new thoughts and possibilities, inviting new benefits into your life (this is where options develop).

Enjoy Today

- **Focusing** – *Small steps* that direct your thoughts toward meaningful action.

- **Learning** – *Small steps* that gather knowledge for future use and to share with others.

- **Breathing** – *Small steps* that energize, calm, restore, and keep you alive.

- **Incidental Movement** – *Small steps* that support your health and add to your exercise.

- **Acknowledging** – *Small steps* that notice and accept your emotions, taking the first step toward understanding and processing them.

- **Clarifying** – *Small steps* that separate fact from fiction and aid in perspective.

- **Communicating** – *Small steps* that seek connections, which offer the benefits of emotional release, different perspectives, and valuable insights.

- **Gratitude** – *Small steps* that recognize being thankful for what you have enhances your overall well-being and deepens your connection to the Universe.

- **Generosity** – *Small steps* that give back, whether through time, resources, or kindness, honoring the gifts you've received while enriching both the giver and receiver.

- ➤ **Belief** – *Small steps* that provide faith and hope on an unseen and unprovable path.

- ➤ **Forgiveness** – *Small steps* that recognize that imperfection is universal and addressing flaws is essential to living.

- ➤ **Priorities** – *Small steps* that provide a clear focus to direct your time toward what truly matters.

- ➤ **Practice** – *Small steps* that, repeated today, lead toward what you want tomorrow.

- ➤ **Persistence** – *Small steps* that move you forward through difficulties and distractions.

- ➤ **Patience** – *Small steps* that remind you that progress often takes longer than expected.

Please reread this list a few times, pausing to consider how you use, or could use, these steps in your everyday life. For example, how could belief aid your priorities? How could focus add to your communication? How could you weave being open into your gratitude?

When needed, you'll find each of these steps can be called on in support of the others.

"When needed" is whenever you recognize that you want things to go better, get better, or simply want to Enjoy Today.

Enjoy Today

Body walks the path.
Thinking clears the way.
Emotions bring your heart.
Time keeps unfolding steps.
Spirit keeps the possibilities.

YOUR THINKING ADDS STRENGTH

"You have power over your mind, not outside events. Realize this, and you will find strength."
—**Marcus Aurelius**

There are countless ways to think, and by intentionally engaging your thinking, you unlock your power to guide yourself, recover from setbacks, and shape the meaning and progress in your life. Time and again, using these three key steps will strengthen your thinking to integrate it with your other strengths:

- **Being Open** – Embracing new thoughts and possibilities to invite new benefits into your life (this is where options develop).

- **Focusing** – Directing your thoughts toward meaningful action.

> **Learning** – Gathering knowledge for future use and to share with others.

Thinkers, over the years, have considered and shared the *"how to's,"* the *"what to's,"* and the *"when to's"* of thinking. One of my favorites, by Henry Ford, is *"Think you can, or think you can't, you're right."*

The idea of cognition has gained popularity as the mental process of using thought. It includes functions like attention, memory, perception, reasoning, and problem-solving. As humans, we're especially vulnerable to a cognitive bias known as anchoring—whether it's past feelings, thoughts of regret, or even old beliefs that no longer serve us, our minds tend to latch on and hold tight. When that works for us, it speeds up decision-making and provides stability. Working against us, it locks us into old patterns and distorts new experiences, even preventing growth.

Here, you'll find ideas for connecting your thinking in the moment to your other strengths. Certainly, how you think is deeply personal and nuanced. You may reflect and analyze before responding. You may think on your feet, relying on instincts or quick emotional cues. Or perhaps you zoom in and go step by step, noticing fine details others miss.

Whatever way you think, remember, while there are logical inconsistencies, if you couple your thinking with your other strengths, you can add to its power. Your thinking can lead you forward to enjoyment and possibility or backward into regret or limitation.

Yes, There Are Practices To Enjoy More

I feel I should mention overthinking, as it is something I often do. At times, I find myself passing the time dwelling on repetitive, non-helpful thoughts. At other times, I need time to think through an issue and surface options. I guess that's not really overthinking, but sometimes it's hard to tell the difference.

However you think, or overthink, here are some thoughts to consider:

- Listening to your thoughts is the first step in guiding them.
- Thinking is not a fixed trait; it can be developed.
- If overthinking is a problem, acknowledging it is the first step to calming it.
- Emotional connections connect your thinking to its power and depth.
- Other people's thoughts influence you, and your thoughts affect them in return.

> Thinking is using your mind and
> giving thought a chance.

BEING OPEN

"An open mind leaves a chance for someone to drop a worthwhile thought in it."
—Mark Twain

We all have learned lessons that may serve us well, and it can be easy to forget, especially as we get older, that other, potentially better practices exist. Here's the truth: being open doesn't mean taking action; it means creating space to receive ideas without judgment. As Aristotle said: "It is the mark of an educated mind to be able to entertain a thought without accepting it."

When thoughts flow freely, it gives you the power to adapt and direct them as you choose. New information and opportunities are ever-evolving, bringing new perspectives and ideas that can transform your life in ways big and small. Staying open can be as straightforward as asking open-ended questions about people, situations, and yourself—and listening to the answers.

Exploring alternate routes on your drive is being open. Watching a movie that someone else wants you to watch is being open. Trying a new exercise instead of, or in addition to, what you've been doing is being open. Sometimes, you find something you enjoy; other times, you return to what you know best.

Routines certainly offer comfort *and* predictability, but sometimes, the ruts they create are limiting. Staying open allows you to see new possibilities, broaden your perspectives, and discover insights that might quietly shape your next steps.

The ability to open, like keeping a window cracked to let in fresh air, is a strength. As you read the following steps, please pause to reflect on how these—and the steps you already practice—are used, or could be used, to connect with and support your other strengths.

SMALL STEPS TO PRACTICE BEING OPEN

1. Ask "why?"
2. Actively listen to answers.
3. Ask follow-up questions or, when talking with others, pause to ask, *"What about you?" "What else?"* or *"What more?"*
4. Say 'yes' instead of 'no.'
5. Make lists of possibilities on paper or in your mind.

ASK YOURSELF

- What would you add to this list?
- What have you thought about bringing into your life?
- Is there a topic you've avoided exploring simply because it feels unfamiliar?
- What have you viewed as an obstacle that might actually be an opportunity?
- Is there a time when being too open is too much?

> "The mind is like a parachute.
> It doesn't work if it is not open."
> **—Frank Zappa**

One more thing: Staying open leads to having options, and that is a key ally in adapting to changing circumstances and situations. Having options matters because they give you the freedom to pick better over good. But of course, not having options is also an option.

Having options is like having a map with multiple possible routes to your destination. It's a strength. As you read the following steps, please pause to reflect on how these—and the steps you already practice—are used, or could be used, to connect with and support your other strengths.

SMALL STEPS TO PRACTICE HAVING OPTIONS

1. More options come from being open.

Enjoy Today

2. More options give you choices.

3. More options can cure feelings of being stuck or lacking energy.

4. A break from routine can help you see new options and fresh perspectives.

5. Have one option for the fun of it :).

6. Have one unconventional option to spark an unexpected solution that would take luck to be accomplished.

7. Share your options with those who might advise you to gain fresh insights, reveal blind spots, and see what you may have overlooked.

8. Instead of saying, *"I can't,"* try saying, *"I can,"* or *"How can I?"*

ASK YOURSELF

➢ What would you add to this list?

➢ What options have you been considering?

➢ Is there an area of your life where new options would be beneficial?

> "Having options is the foundation of autonomy and self-determination."
> **—Malcolm Gladwell**

FOCUSING

Think more about what you want—
and less about what you don't want.

Focus, ultimately, is your tool for minimizing distractions. Whether instinctively or intentionally, it enables you to pay more attention to fewer things—in other words, to keep your eye on the ball. This allows some doors to remain unopened and paths remain unexplored for another time.

That said, there are many interesting and entertaining distractions. They're not necessarily bad, just distractions from what I think I want to be doing, yet sometimes a distraction is exactly what I need: a break. You?

Being open and having options supports distractions.

When you want to take action, focus supports you to do so.

"What are you paying attention to?" is the core question that shapes focus.

Focusing will help you sustain your attention, ease the pressure, and guide your efforts in the direction you have chosen, whether it's education, relaxation, a task, a goal, or an idea.

The ability to focus, like an archer locking onto a target, is a strength. As you read the following steps, please pause to reflect on how these—and the steps you already practice—are used, or could be used, to connect and support your other strengths.

SMALL STEPS TO PRACTICE FOCUSING

1. Focus on what you want in your life.
2. If you're unsure, revisit the steps of being open and having options.
3. Minimize distractions by moving to a quieter environment, switching your phone to 'Do Not Disturb,' and closing any distracting apps.
4. Where you focus goes, your energy will flow.
5. Use personal cues, such as blinking your eyes, rolling your head, or taking deep breaths, to remind yourself it's time to focus.
6. Consciously focusing on solutions will give you more energy.
7. Take breaks to help you sustain focus.
8. Don't focus on what went wrong; focus on making it right.

9. Celebrate small wins to reinforce your focus, motivation, and movement.

10. If you burn out, take a break from focusing for a while.

ASK YOURSELF

- What would you add to this list?
- What techniques do you use for focusing?
- Are there things you've wanted to accomplish but haven't?
- Have you focused on them?

> "Focus is a matter of deciding what things you're not going to do."
> **—John Carmack**

LEARNING

"The capacity to learn is a gift; the ability
to learn is a skill; the willingness to learn
is a choice."
—**Brian Herbert**

Learning is the process of acquiring experiences and insights to gain new perspectives and open new possibilities. It goes well beyond formal education, and you can focus on and learn in any area you choose.

As you open, explore options, and focus, you'll gain insights into what works, what works best, and what doesn't work at all. These lessons help you build emotional strength and flexibility, enabling you to view setbacks as learning opportunities.

To foster learning at any time, including right now, pause and ask yourself three questions: *What am I learning? Do I want to learn more about it? What else do I want to learn?*

Sometimes, your lessons will be clear—you know when something clicks or a misstep occurs. Other times, insights might emerge unexpectedly, during a walk, in the shower, or through casual conversation. Staying receptive to these moments and being willing to pause, reflect, and absorb the lesson is a key to learning.

The ability to learn, like a torch lighting the way in darkness, is a strength. As you read the following steps, please pause to reflect on how these—and the steps you already practice—are used, or could be used, to connect with and support your other strengths.

SMALL STEPS TO PRACTICE LEARNING

1. Learning involves being open and listening.
2. Feedback is an important part of learning.
3. Make comments and listen to responses.
4. Take a moment after any activity to ask yourself if there's something to be learned, and listen to your answers.
5. Ask yourself and others: *What's going well? What could be improved?*
6. To reinforce your understanding, teach others.
7. Do what you don't know: The more you do, the more you will learn.

8. "The more you know, the more you know you don't know."

ASK YOURSELF

➢ What would you add to this list?

➢ What lessons have been most important to you?

➢ Are there two or three lessons that you regularly share with others?

➢ What do you look forward to learning?

➢ Have you learned to enjoy your life?

> "The most difficult part of adult learning is choosing to learn."
> **—Seth Godin**

YOUR BODY ADDS STRENGTH

"Your body is an instrument, not an ornament."
—Unknown

Author Jim Rohn said, *"Take care of your body; it's the only place you have to live."* This reality has fueled countless programs designed to keep the body working well and build its strength, stamina, endurance, flexibility, and appearance.

Your body is one of a kind. It holds unique capabilities, quiet strengths, and natural limits. There are endless body types and just as many ways to support them. And while what's inside will always matter most, your physical body is the visible expression of your vitality—your health, your strength, and even your confidence.

When your body is cared for, it becomes a source of power and energy. When it's ignored or depleted, everything feels harder. Good health is not a mystery. It's built, step by step, with things that are simple but often overlooked: restful sleep, a nourishing diet, daily movement, hydration, and taking care of yourself before problems begin. These practices don't require perfection—only presence. They're quiet acts of support that keep your body working well and help you feel more at ease in your own skin.

Among all the steps you can take, two stand out for their simplicity, power, and their ability to support you and your other personal strengths: mindful breathing and incremental movement. Both are free. Both are available at any time. Though these actions may seem small, they hold great impact—if you choose them.

> **Mindful Breathing** – Every mindful breath is a reminder: you are here, you are safe, and this moment is yours.

> **Incidental Movement** – To supplement your other activities. Exercise is great, yet in the moment, there is always another opportunity to move your body.

A single breath can calm your nerves.
Add energy with a stretch, a bend,
or standing up for a moment.

MINDFUL BREATHING

The first step of breath—is simply to notice it.

Mindful Breathing is power. Awareness of your breath has the potential to transform your daily experiences and heighten your abilities, including your capacity to move through difficulties and to enjoy moments. Ignoring the opportunity to breathe means missing out on a powerful ally in navigating daily challenges and opportunities.

The breath is your constant companion that can guide you moment by moment. Unlike other vital functions, breathing is unique: it happens automatically, yet you can also control it consciously. Practicing conscious breathing is a *small step* to living more fully in the present moment and connecting to the needs of your other strengths.

Using your breath, like a bridge connecting your body and mind, is a strength. As you read the following steps, please pause to reflect on how these—and the steps you already practice—are used, or could be used, in connecting and supporting your other strengths.

SMALL STEPS TO PRACTICE BREATHING

1. Notice your natural breathing rhythm without altering it.
2. Breathe through your nose so you become more conscious of it.
3. Become mindful of your inhales, holds, and exhales as the basis of conscious breathing; many call it breathwork.
4. Use planned breathing patterns (inhales, holds, and exhales), which can provide many benefits, including relieving discomfort and stress and energizing action.
5. Try breathwork patterns, like 4-4-4 (inhale-hold-exhale) for calmness, 1-1 (inhale-exhale) for energy, or 4-7-8 for sleep.
6. Create your own breathwork practices.
7. Take a few inhales and exhales to help calm bewilderment, frustration, or anger.
8. Support your movement in any physical activity with breathing.
9. Use your breath to enhance your focus and prepare your muscles for action.

ASK YOURSELF

- What would you add to this list?
- How have you consciously used breathing in your life?
- Do you call on your breath in moments of need and opportunity?
- Do you have breathwork practices?

> "When the breath is steady and controlled,
> the mind is still and calm."
> **—B.K.S. Iyengar**

INCIDENTAL MOVEMENT

Move it or lose it.

Our bodies thrive on—and are built for—movement. In addition to its obvious benefits, it clears the mind and stabilizes emotions, likely due to the increased oxygen flow and mental break it provides.

The most widely practiced form of movement is exercise. It's typically planned, structured, and goal-oriented, it emphasizes duration, intensity, and repetition, and it usually requires specialized equipment or specific locations. Whatever the approach, the healthiest bodies are, at least in part, a result of regular exercise.

However, consider this: in addition to exercise, there is *incidental movement*, which offers multiple benefits and can be easily incorporated into your daily activities. It is unplanned, doesn't require specialized equipment or places, and can be done whenever you think about it, anytime and anywhere. Everyone already does some type of incidental movement throughout their day, and my suggestion is to do it more regularly, more intentionally.

The opportunities are everywhere. Simple actions like standing up from a chair, intentionally walking down a hallway, reaching overhead, touching your toes, twisting your torso from one side to the other, and rolling your shoulders are all forms of incidental movement.

When you're stiff from exercise, or your body's calling for more, incidental movement can be called on. When you hear yourself saying, *"I don't like to exercise,"* it's a hint to do incidental movement. When conditions or age limit exercise options, incidental movement is available. When physical difficulties limit exercise, incidental movement is still available.

Using incidental movement, like the slow turning of a wheel forward, is a strength. As you read the following steps, please pause to reflect on how these—and the steps you already practice—are used, or could be used, to connect with and support your other strengths.

SMALL STEPS TO PRACTICE INCIDENTAL MOVEMENT

1. Even now, as you read this, find the opportunity for incidental movement: roll your shoulders, move your head back and forth and around, pull your shoulder blades together, and sit up straighter. Whatever movement might come to mind, give it a try.

Yes, There Are Practices To Enjoy More

2. When you think to yourself, *"I feel stiff"* or *"I need more exercise,"* you're reminding yourself of an opportunity for incidental movement.

3. Add an inch to your step when walking for short periods to add incidental movement to your legs. (It's also a form of interval training.)

4. Throughout the day, before stiffness sets in, pause to stretch. It's a way of using incidental movement—enjoy.

5. Stretch one part of your body. It can lead to incidental movements to stretch other parts of your body.

6. Everyday routines are opportunities for incidental movement. While brushing your teeth, do calf raises. During TV breaks, try light stretching or standing exercises. While standing in line, circle your hips or lean forward or backward. The possibilities are endless.

7. How about now? Take a moment to raise your arms over your head, move your toes up and down, bend over and gently roll up, look right and then left, or pull your shoulders up and down or back and forth. Do whatever comes to mind.

8. Make incidental movement part of your day. It will make you feel better.

ASK YOURSELF
> What would you add to this list?

Enjoy Today

- ➢ Do you get enough movement in your day?
- ➢ Have you considered the value of adding incidental movement?
- ➢ What small movements or stretches do you most enjoy?
- ➢ Why not do them right now?

> A body at rest tends to stay at rest.
> A body in motion tends to stay in motion.

YOUR EMOTION ADDS STRENGTH

> "Let's not forget that the little emotions
> are the great captains of our lives, and
> we obey them without realizing it."
> —**Vincent Van Gogh**

Emotions are the ever-present heartbeat of life, shaping your perceptions and experiences. These feelings can be rational or irrational, uplifting or painful, and are often triggered by the simplest moments. They remind us of our humanity and are early indicators of how we interpret situations and respond.

When positive, emotions enhance enjoyment and resilience; when negative, they can create obstacles rooted in fear and anxiety. To get them out and better understand them, there are three small steps that can be used over and over again to better connect with emotions in support of other personal strengths:

- **Acknowledging** – Noticing and accepting your emotions is the first step toward understanding and processing them.

- **Clarifying** – Differentiating between reality and imagination helps establish perspective and distinguish fact from fiction.

- **Communicating** – Seeking connections offers the benefits of emotional release, additional perspectives, and valuable insights.

Many of us are conditioned to approach emotions cautiously, as though they require careful management and are better not shared. Standards of politeness, caution, and past trauma have taught us to suppress our feelings.

Allowing emotions to be expressed and processed is part of our overall well-being. Whether real or imagined, helpful or challenging, emotions fuel your passions, fears, and satisfactions while connecting you to yourself, others, and the world around you.

Emotions are a universal human experience, and even *small steps* in understanding them can bring significant benefits. Hearing what your emotions are saying can fuel your goals and empower you to overcome challenges. There's a wide network of doctors, therapists, and support groups out there, standing ready to support your emotional needs.

- Emotions bring power and energy to your life.

- ➢ Expressing your emotions can lead to a better understanding of their messages.
- ➢ Holding back your emotions can lead to higher stress and negatively impact your health.
- ➢ Chronic emotional suppression is linked to physical and mental health issues.
- ➢ Emotions such as disappointment and regret offer valuable lessons for personal growth.

Emotions are connecting you with your heart.

ACKNOWLEDGING

Acknowledging emotions validates your experiences, reinforcing that your feelings are real and worthy of attention.

Emotions are the first clues to what's happening around you and how you might respond. Often triggered by a mix of past experiences and present circumstances, they can pass quickly or linger. Acknowledging what they are is a first step to using them. Ignoring them can create cycles of frustration and self-blame, pushing you away from Enjoy Today.

I realized long ago that giving my feelings the attention they deserved was one way of not getting stuck in them. Stuck includes cycles of *"I'm not good enough," "Why me?"* and *"Why don't they like me?"* Over time, I keep learning that it's important for me to get it out—to get on with it, or get over it. Connecting with my emotions hasn't made challenges any easier, but it's made the path ahead clearer, and I've become better equipped to handle difficulties with resilience.

Acknowledging emotions—to enjoy more and work through challenges and setbacks—is a strength. As you read the following steps, please pause to reflect on how these—and the steps you already practice—are used, or could be used, to connect and support your other strengths.

SMALL STEPS TO PRACTICE ACKNOWLEDGING

1. The first step to resolving fear, worry, or anger is acknowledging it.
2. Generally, if you're mad, get it out to get over it.
3. Be your own supportive listener.
4. Generally, if you're happy, enjoy it, share it, and then get on with it.
5. Embrace positive emotions, such as joy, happiness, or success, to fuel well-being.
6. Start with "*I feel* . . ." when sharing emotions, as this emphasizes that it is your own experience and can help you avoid blaming or accusing others.
7. "*I feel . . .*" allows you to take more responsibility for your emotions.
8. Write out your feelings (in W4G, for example) to provide an additional perspective on what you're feeling and allow you to take a pause.

9. Always remember, it will feel better in the morning. Time is an elixir.

ASK YOURSELF

- ➢ What else would you add to this list?
- ➢ How have your emotions guided you?
- ➢ What two emotions have been difficult to share?
- ➢ How else would you have processed them?
- ➢ How would you advise others to use their emotions?

> "It's intriguing; when I acknowledge myself just as I am, I can change."
> **—Carl Rogers**

CLARIFYING

Close as we are
We've never been so far
The tide stays high
But the sadness is exposed

Some emotions are straightforward and easy to trace, while others lie hidden beneath layers of overthinking, denial, or unresolved past experiences. Without clarifying these hidden emotions, they can remain confusing, leaving you stuck in cycles of negativity or wondering why. Clarifying requires peeling back layers to get to the heart of what's genuinely affecting you.

Identifying the root causes of your feelings can help you gain insight into your emotional patterns and break free from reactions based on misunderstandings. It can also help you understand why you feel a certain way and give you better access to the tools that help you respond more effectively.

Enjoy Today

Clarifying, like a puzzle where each piece finally falls into place, is a strength. As you read the following steps, please pause to reflect on how these—and the steps you already practice—are used, or could be used, to connect and support your other strengths.

SMALL STEPS TO PRACTICE CLARIFYING

1. Take a few deep breaths.

2. Consider the source of the emotion. Is it from a recent event, an old memory, or an ongoing concern?

3. If the source is not immediately apparent, searching for it may provide further insights, direction, and options.

4. Ask yourself: *"What's driving these feelings?" "What events or thoughts are triggering them?"*

5. Slow things down with deep inhales and exhales to bring new insights and clarity.

6. Take the time to reflect without rushing to conclusions, as this can also provide valuable insights.

7. Take a walk, take a break, or spend time in nature to create emotional distance from your feelings and gain a different perspective.

8. Do some physical activity, which helps process emotions and release tension.

Yes, There Are Practices To Enjoy More

9. Talk through your feelings with someone you trust, as this can reveal things you might not have seen on your own.

ASK YOURSELF

- ➢ What would you add to this list?
- ➢ How have you clarified your emotions?
- ➢ What advice would you offer others to see things more clearly?

"When we clarify our emotions, we are no longer at their mercy. We become empowered to choose how to move forward."
—Susan David

COMMUNICATING

"Shared joy is a double joy; shared sorrow is a half sorrow."
—Swedish Proverb

The above proverb holds weight and stems from the fact that, as social beings, we have an innate need for connection and a sense of belonging. When things are going well, enjoying the moments with others increases our appreciation. When things are going poorly (with problems, worries, or overwhelm), we may fear that others might judge, dismiss, or misunderstand us, which can stifle emotions.

The benefits of communicating your emotions include gaining new perspectives, increasing your understanding, and reminding yourself that you are not alone in your experiences. This lyric from David Crosby reminds me that there are verbal and nonverbal ways to communicate: *"If you smile at me, I will understand, 'cause that is something everybody everywhere does in the same language."*

That said, communicating with others is not always easy. Many of us have not been taught how to identify, label, and express our emotions effectively. This lack of "emotional literacy" can make it difficult to understand what we're feeling, let alone communicate it.

Yes, it's easier to communicate in supportive and non-judgmental environments, but we may still be hesitant to trust and share our feelings. Maybe we don't trust who we're talking with, haven't had role models who communicated, or perhaps a lack of listening gets in the way of knowing what to say.

Societal expectations can discourage emotional expression. For example, men may feel pressured to suppress their emotions or believe that expressing certain emotions is "inappropriate." No matter who you are, sharing negative or positive emotions might feel uncomfortable because it exposes your innermost thoughts and feelings.

To fill this need for communication, there is a wide variety of professional help offering diagnosis, treatment, and prevention. Contacting online groups, therapists, and doctors who specialize in emotional health can all be beneficial.

Communicating with others, like building a bridge across a divide, is a strength. As you read the following steps, please pause to reflect on how these—and the steps you already practice—are used, or could be used, to connect with and support your other strengths.

SMALL STEPS TO PRACTICE COMMUNICATING

1. Choose the right time. Pick a time when you can communicate honestly and listening isn't challenged by other activities.

2. Choose the right place. A calm, private moment offers a better time for an open and honest conversation than a hectic situation or a public setting.

3. Make eye contact.

4. When sharing is difficult, phrases like *"I feel"* or *"I've been feeling"* keep the focus on your experience and may allow a more open discussion about the underlying issue or subject.

5. Describe your emotions specifically rather than generalizing, as this improves clarity and understanding. For example, instead of saying, *"I'm upset,"* try, *"I'm upset because . . ."*

6. In a world full of opinions, there is no need to respond to all comments.

7. Carefully listen to others to gain their insights and show you value the person's thoughts and feelings.

8. After an emotional conversation or meeting, follow up with the person later to reinforce trust in the relationship.

9. Sharing isn't a weakness; it's a *small step* that becomes a big step toward emotional growth.

ASK YOURSELF

- What would you add to this list?
- Have you found ways to comfortably share your emotions?
- Is there someone you need to communicate with more often?

To support emotional clarity and self-awareness, Enjoy Today offers several helpful practices. Try the following approaches:

- Use W4G as a way to explore your thoughts and feelings.
- Speak kindly to yourself, especially in difficult times.
- Guide yourself in positive directions.
- Direct your self-talk to protect and strengthen your emotional energy.
- Inspire yourself to motivate you and direct your steps.
- Call on your body to lift your mood.
- Build personal strengths to respond to challenges and opportunities.

> "Feelings are much like waves; we can't stop them from coming, but we can choose which one to surf."
> —**Jonatan Mårtensson**

YOUR SPIRIT ADDS STRENGTH

> "There is a force in the universe, which, if we permit it, will flow through us and produce miraculous results."
> **—Mahatma Gandhi**

Recognizing the vastness and complexity of creation can inspire a sense of wonder, humility, and a deeper understanding. Noticing that we are all interconnected parts of a greater whole can foster empathy and compassion. While there are limitless opportunities to connect with that creation, four steps are consistently useful in helping you access and invite the Spirit into your life. Coincidently, they are also fundamental to all major religions:

- ➢ **Gratitude** – Recognizing and being thankful for what you have enhances your overall well-being and deepens your connection to the Universe.

- ➢ **Generosity** – Giving back, whether through time, resources, or kindness, honors the gifts you've received while enriching both the giver and receiver.

- ➢ **Belief** – Faith and hope for something unseen and unprovable provide comfort, purpose, and connection on an unknown path.

- ➢ **Forgiveness** – Recognizing that imperfection is universal and addressing flaws is essential to living.

The most brilliant minds have only scratched at the surface of the Universe. Joni Mitchell observed so beautifully that *"We are stardust,"* Albert Einstein formulated relativity *($E=mc^2$)*, and Stephen Hawking sought to explain complex theories like the Big Bang and quantum mechanics.

What is clear beyond a doubt is that humans did not create the Universe's underlying intelligence and grand design. It is the natural, unexplainable creation of everything. You may call it God, Spirit, Universe, Creator, or a Higher Power, or perhaps you choose not to recognize it at all.

Still.

Whatever this power is, it's a vast, unseen universe beyond human comprehension.

Whatever this power is, it shifts you away from your sense of importance.

Whatever this power is, it can't be fully explained, proven, or seen.

Whatever this power is, it has to be believed, and what I wrote above is what I believe.

Over millennia, organized religions have provided rules, rituals, and prayers to connect with this power. Yet it's worth remembering that this unseen force existed long before religions gave it a name or a structure.

Reflecting on the eternal nature of Spirit can offer a sense of peace and tranquility, providing comfort during difficult times. Seeing the mysteries of the Universe can spark creativity and imagination by encouraging the exploration of new ideas and possibilities.

How the small steps of Spirit manifest in your life is uniquely personal. It may involve prayer, meditation, study, a walk in nature, or simply contemplating its mysteries. Ultimately, your belief in this "grand design" is more important than the specific path you follow.

- Spirit reminds us that each being, thought, and action is part of a grand design.
- Spirit transcends our physical world to one existing beyond time and space.
- Spirit offers connections that defy human limitations.
- Spirit opens possibilities beyond logic, yielding more profound truths.
- Spirit can come from deep connections or flashes in the moment.

Enjoy Today

Spirit brings the wonder of the
Universe into your life.

GRATITUDE

"Be thankful for what you have, and you'll end up having more. If you focus on what you don't have, you'll never have enough."
—**Oprah Winfrey**

Focusing on what you're thankful for helps shift your attention from what you lack to what you appreciate. It allows you to enjoy what you already have, deepening your appreciation of what you've been given and attracting more of what you want into your life.

By actively practicing gratitude, you recognize the positive. Each moment of thankfulness allows you to see the good in everyday interactions and experiences, which can transform your outlook and improve your overall well-being.

You can be thankful for anything in your life—including life itself. Even during challenging times, acknowledging what you're grateful for can help you navigate difficulties with renewed hope. Identifying what you're not grateful for can highlight areas for improvement to guide your next steps.

Gratitude in life, like a muscle that grows stronger with use, is a strength. As you read the following steps, please pause to reflect on how these—and the steps you already practice—are used, or could be used, to connect with and support your other strengths.

SMALL STEPS TO PRACTICE GRATITUDE

1. Be thankful for opinions, service, time, and the contributions of others. It's a small, free act that fosters appreciation in both you and the other person.

2. Say thank you.

3. Pause in the moments of your day to recognize and enjoy even the smallest actions, conditions, or events you are grateful for. Say thank you.

4. Make a conscious effort to reframe challenges and identify their positive aspects and lessons, and be grateful for that ability. Say thank you.

5. When facing difficulties, seek out the hidden blessings they often come with, offering growth and new perspectives. Say thank you.

6. Today, tell someone what you enjoy about them or their positive impact on your life. Do it every day, and gratitude will grow. Say thank you.

7. Be fully present when enjoying a meal, a conversation, or a quiet moment to acknowledge how fortunate you are experiencing it. Say thank you.

8. Recognize that, compared to others, you have many blessings to be thankful for.

9. Keep in your mind, or on paper, a list of what you're grateful for and refer to it regularly. Say thank you.

ASK YOURSELF

➤ What would you add to this list?

➤ Have you made a list of what you are grateful for?

➤ How often do you reflect on it?

➤ Are there challenges to your being grateful?

➤ Would you like to enjoy more?

With a grateful heart, you will attract
more you are grateful for.

GENEROSITY

"You don't have to be an angel to act like one."
—Mort Schapiro

In a world where differences are often highlighted, generosity brings us closer together, focusing on what unites us rather than what sets us apart. Giving to others breaks down barriers, dissolves judgments, and reminds us of our shared humanity. It's a powerful antidote to negativity and narrow-minded thinking.

People witnessing generosity are often moved to be more generous themselves, continuing to spread the benefits of giving and creating cycles of positive energy that bring unity and connection.

Life is a gift, and as we receive it, we also benefit by giving back to others. There are many ways to be generous, from offering a smile to providing time, attention, or kindness.

Generosity, like a tree offering shade and fruit to all, is a strength rooted in kindness. As you read the following steps, please pause to reflect on how these—and the steps you already practice—are used, or could be used, to connect with and support your other strengths.

SMALL STEPS TO PRACTICE GENEROSITY

1. Smile. It's a simple, free generosity that shares with you and others the goodness in small moments.

2. Recognize that there is generosity in offering words of support and encouragement to those who are having difficulties (including yourself).

3. Send a quick message. A simple recognition can let people know you see and believe in them.

4. GIVE BIGGER TIPS: Surprise and delight recipients with generosity that exceeds their expectations, leaving a positive and lasting impact.

5. Offer simple, unexpected acts of generosity. This could include buying coffee for a stranger, holding the door open, or offering comments of encouragement.

6. Recognize someone's talents and contributions. This is a generosity that can boost confidence, uplift spirits, and make them (and you) feel seen and valued.

7. Support causes that you care about.

8. Lighten someone's day. Anytime you can do this, it's an opportunity to be generous.

ASK YOURSELF

- What would you add to this list?
- Have you experienced the benefits of generosity?
- What gifts have you been given?
- Have you given those gifts to others?
- Do you believe that the more you give, the more you get?

> "We make a living by what we get,
> but we make a life by what we give."
> **—Winston Churchill**

BELIEF

"A belief is not merely an idea the mind
possesses; it is an idea that possesses the mind."
—**Robert Oxton Bolton**

While belief and doubt are powerful forces, belief is the one that provides the courage and confidence to take the next step. It counters the fear of the unknown and encourages you to keep moving forward, even when results aren't immediately obvious. Belief offers hope and faith in results you can't yet see.

Often linked with religion, belief has great value in everyday life. You believe your loved ones will return safely from a trip, children will come home from school, you will get that new offer, and your community will recover from difficult times. Belief reassures you that, despite uncertainty, good things can and will happen.

"This too shall pass." It's normal to question belief, especially when life gets hard, but that's when belief becomes even more essential. Knowing that difficult moments may linger but are temporary is when belief becomes a guiding force.

Belief, like a sail that catches the wind to move you forward, is a strength. As you read the following steps, please pause to reflect on how these—and the steps you already practice—are used, or could be used, to connect with and support your other strengths.

SMALL STEPS TO PRACTICE BELIEF

1. Belief in yourself is one of the most powerful beliefs, and it is one that you control.

2. Close your eyes. Visualize things turning out all right.

3. Imagine positive outcomes to reinforce the belief that good things are possible.

4. Remember: Light always follows dark, spring always follows winter, and endings always come with new beginnings.

5. Believe in better days. It gives you the strength to move through the bad days.

6. Develop positive habits and routines to reinforce your belief in yourself.

7. Spend time with people whose honesty and encouragement reinforce your belief in yourself. Spend less time with those who don't.

8. If worry and doubt swirl, belief offers you a foundation of trust that your efforts will bear fruit.

ASK YOURSELF

- What would you add to this list?
- What core beliefs have made you stronger?
- How have you brought belief into your life?
- What's more important—belief or luck?

> "Faith is a knowledge within the heart, beyond the reach of proof."
> **—Kahlil Gibran**

FORGIVENESS

"To forgive is to set a prisoner free and discover that the prisoner was you."
—Lewis B. Smedes

There will be times when things go wrong. Maybe you've made a mistake, or you're confronted with the actual or perceived mistakes or slights of others. The first step toward letting go of anger and blame is recognizing that nothing is perfect, that setbacks are inevitable, and that you and others are flawed.

Everyone makes mistakes, especially those who achieve a lot.

Forgiveness means releasing yourself to move on. It creates space for "next time" and that second or third chance when your humanity and resilience come into play. It's about a mindset that allows for growth and learning.

Don't want to forgive? OK. Moving forward, perhaps a question to ask yourself is, *"What am I getting from not forgiving?"* or *"How is not forgiving adding enjoyment to my life?"*

Forgiveness, like turning the page in a book, allows you to move on with the story, and it is a strength. As you read the following steps, please pause to reflect on how these—and the steps you already practice—are used, or could be used, to connect with and support your other strengths.

***SMALL STEPS* TO PRACTICE FORGIVENESS**

1. Let go of self-blame, as it is a step towards personal compassion and resilience. Perhaps it also opens the door to forgiving others.

2. Say *"I'm sorry"* to show that you recognize your actions or words had an impact instead of ignoring or dismissing them.

3. Practice generosity and gratitude to focus on the positive aspects of relationships and situations, cultivate empathy, and help release resentment.

4. Let go of minor frustrations or annoyances. It will strengthen your ability to move on, and over time, this practice will make room for you to enjoy more.

5. Understand another point of view, as it can make forgiveness easier.

6. Focus on the present and let go of mistakes and perceived wrongs to open the door to enjoying more.

7. If you can't forgive others, forgive yourself and move on.

ASK YOURSELF

- ➤ What would you add to this list?
- ➤ Is there someone you've thought about forgiving?
- ➤ What is holding you back?
- ➤ Is there something for which you would ask for forgiveness?

> "Ring the bells that still can ring.
> Forget your perfect offering.
> There is a crack in everything.
> That's how the light gets in."
> **—Leonard Cohen**

TIME ADDS STRENGTH

Everything worthwhile takes time.
Often more time than expected.

Using the time you have right now is the best way to support all your other strengths.

Time isn't an abstract thing that slips away; it's the agent that empowers everything. The truth is, it's not about how much time you have; it's about how you use time. It's you that matters. It's not time that matters. Time is not waiting; it's not slowing down, and unlike other resources, it's non-renewable.

There are countless ways to shape time in your favor, from reflecting and adjusting to pausing and pushing. Yet, for me, time and again, four steps interweave with your other strengths to consistently help make your moments work for you:

> **Prioritize.** Setting your priorities provides a clear focus to direct your time toward what truly matters.

Enjoy Today

- **Practice.** Repeating *small steps* today leads toward what you want tomorrow.
- **Persist.** Persistence is what moves you forward through difficulties and distractions.
- **Be Patient.** Patience reminds you that progress often takes longer than expected.

Time is always on your side. Until it isn't.

What if time isn't something to find but something you already have, waiting for you to notice? What if it's less about running out of time and more about how you engage with your moments? Time's not out of reach—it's right here, today. The question is: How are you going to use it?

The past? Sure, it's the background of your life, and it has taught you many lessons. Some you liked, some you didn't.

The future? Yeah, that's where your life will go, and shaping it will only be done by the thoughts, actions, and beliefs you have today.

Today is the space between your past and the future and where your life happens. Your choices here shape everything, and you are the one that makes them. If you're stuck thinking about what's already behind you or dreaming about what's ahead, you may be missing the power of the present time right in front of you.

> Today is a gift; that's why they call it the present.

Yes, There Are Practices To Enjoy More

Here's the thing: How you handle today, this moment, will determine your next moments, and the next ones, and the next ones, and then one after another, how you enjoy your life. Worrying about what others are doing or saying about you is wasting your time, and your time will soon be gone.

- Today is your only opportunity to take action.
- Today is the only place you can enjoy what you have.
- Today is the only time you can learn from yesterday.
- Today is the only path to guide yourself to tomorrow.
- Today is where you decline, progress, or discover new paths.
- Today is where you can let the benefits of life outweigh the burdens.
- When there is "no time," you still have time.
- When you run out of time, you run out of opportunity—at least in this life.
- Enjoy Today because everything can change tomorrow.

> "Time is the most valuable thing
> a man can spend."
> **—Theophrastus**

If you had yesterday to do over (you don't), how would you apply that to today?

PRIORITIES

Priorities aren't just what we list.
They're what we do, choose,
and invest our time in daily.

Your personal priorities may whisper or shout. If you're paying attention to them, you're heading in the right direction. They are the points of a compass that can guide you in your direction of choice.

Sure, interruptions or obligations conflict with what might really matter to you, but the truth that no one tells you is that personal priorities don't play by the rules. Are you paying attention to them, or are you too busy juggling everything else? It's easy to do. Separating life's obligations and comforts from personal priorities is difficult, and life can be too messy to organize everything neatly.

Compartmentalization is a quick fix. I've done it, and it's worked, but perhaps it's not the solution. By allowing your priorities and passions to overlap naturally with your obligations, I believe you'll enjoy both more.

Using priorities, like a spotlight that illuminates what truly matters, is a strength. As you read the following steps, please pause to reflect on how these—and the steps you already practice—are used, or could be used, to connect with and support your other strengths.

SMALL STEPS TO PRACTICE PRIORITIES

1. Prioritize. When you spend time with loved ones, they're the priority. When you spend time alone, you're the priority. When you're at work, it's the priority.

2. Make a to-do list. Put "A's" by your priorities and "B's" by the others. Move forward with the "A's and cross off the "B's." Repeat as needed.

3. Make a not-to-do list. Highlight distractions, unnecessary tasks, or habits that derail your focus so you can avoid them.

4. Say no to commitments that don't align with your direction.

5. Say yes to opportunities that take you in the direction of your priorities.

6. Acknowledge progress on your priorities by celebrating small wins.

7. Set aside time every day to focus on things that matter most.

ASK YOURSELF

- What would you add to this list?
- Do your priorities overlap with your obligations?
- Could your priorities overlap with your obligations?
- Is there a priority you've forgotten about?

> "The key is not to prioritize what's on your schedule, but to schedule your priorities."
> —**Stephen Covey**

PRACTICE

Practice when the stakes are low—
to be prepared when the stakes are high.

Through practice, today's priorities and repetition meet. Practice is where small steps go from difficult to easier, and not wanting to shifts to enjoyment. It's through practice that true change takes root and grows. It's through practice that you begin to notice what you're good at, what you can improve, and what you're doing wrong—so you can work on making it right.

Practice and repetition are the foundations of growth. Transforming *small steps* into meaningful progress. Each time you repeat an action, you build skill, resilience, and understanding. Over time, these small, consistent efforts accumulate, transforming intentions into habits and wishes into reality.

Embrace the power of doing it again, knowing the first steps can be difficult but are always the path to the next steps—and, eventually, to arriving at the results you desire.

Practice, like repeatedly polishing a stone to reveal its brilliance, is a strength. As you read the following steps, please pause to reflect on how these—and the steps you already practice—are used, or could be used, to connect with and support your other strengths.

SMALL STEPS TO PRACTICE

1. Gain clarity. The more specifically you see and enjoy the benefits you're working toward, the more effectively you'll practice.

2. Listen and learn. These are key tools in building and guiding your practices.

3. Expect resistance. Not wanting to do something is normal; keep reminding yourself you will enjoy it when the practice is over.

4. Don't stop. When it's tiring, you'll know you're on the right track.

5. Some do practice for perfection and most practice for growth; both are great.

6. Add time and technique as your repetition and engagement grow.

7. Expect to feel good when practice is complete, and congratulate yourself for taking another step.

8. Remember that when you decide not to practice something, you are moving on. What's next is something that will also require practice.

9. Don't let the buzzards get you down.

ASK YOURSELF

- ➢ What would you add to this list?
- ➢ What would you like to get better at?
- ➢ Are you practicing?
- ➢ What's holding you back?

> "Practice is the best of all instructors."
> **—Publilius Syrus**

PERSISTENCE

"A river cuts through rock, not because of its power, but because of its persistence."
—**James N. Watkins**

The myth of easy results and overnight success is a persuasive one. Yet, there will be ups and downs, setbacks, and distractions along your path. Persistence will keep you moving forward and bouncing back when hitches, difficulties, or failures threaten to pull you off-course.

When you have an end in mind, these moments of pushing through create something almost magical, turning effort into momentum. As you persist, remember to celebrate small victories; they add up and remind you why you began.

In persisting, you take the next *small steps*—despite obstacles—to gain invaluable insights. You find that mistakes contain the seeds for learning skills and sharpening resilience.

In the end, success is found not only in the outcome but in the growth and character you forge through the persistence to reach it.

Persistence, like a rising tide steadily lifting all that comes before it, is a strength. As you read the following steps, please pause to reflect on how these—and the steps you already practice—are used, or could be used, to connect with and support your other strengths.

SMALL STEPS TO PRACTICE PERSISTENCE

1. Use W4G to gain perspective that will help you shape, guide, clarify, and take action where you want to persist.

2. In the face of challenges, take a moment, close your eyes, and visualize what you'll achieve.

3. Have an "end in mind" to guide your steps and to distinguish the long term from the short term.

4. Seek encouragement and advice from those who support your direction.

5. Allow input from those who don't support your direction. See it as resistance to break through and to determine what else you might need to consider.

6. Understand that steps backward are just part of moving forward.

7. Use PTR to REfresh, REnew, and REimagine your persistence.

8. Remember that persistence is the fuel of progress. If you're not making progress, perhaps you're uncovering new and more rewarding paths.

ASK YOURSELF

- ➢ What would you add to this list?
- ➢ What strengths have you found in persisting?
- ➢ Have you persisted in what's important to you?
- ➢ What would you offer to others to aid their persistence?
- ➢ Is there a time to stop persisting?

> "It's not that I'm so smart; it's just that I stay with problems longer."
> **—Albert Einstein**

PATIENCE

"Everything takes time—many times
more time than you think."
—**Morgan Harper Nichols**

Patience helps you be calm and focused while waiting for results or dealing with setbacks. Often viewed as a passive virtue, patience is, in fact, an active and strategic tool that can significantly impact your outcomes. It allows you to step back from the immediate situation so you can gain a broader perspective to inform your decisions, review progress, and decide when it's better to wait.

In a world that often demands immediate action, it's valuable to understand when a brief respite can lead to better results. With patience, you can review progress, identify patterns, and determine the next steps to take. Patience may allow opportunities to mature, obstacles to dissipate, or new information to emerge that could significantly influence your approach.

Enjoy Today

Overnight success is a myth.

Persistence is closely related to patience because both involve, over time, enduring challenges and staying committed to a direction or goal. Both bridge the space between effort and reward, spanning the gap between time and uncertainty.

Patience, like a sculptor chipping away slowly to reveal something beautiful, is a strength. As you read the following steps, please pause to reflect on how these—and the steps you already practice—are used, or could be used, to connect with and support your other strengths.

SMALL STEPS TO PRACTICE PATIENCE

1. Remember that when it takes longer than expected, it's to be expected.

2. Know that slow goes hand in hand with fast. They complement each other, and both add value.

3. See that slowing down can lead to speeding up, and vice versa.

4. Don't forget the natural process of seeds growing into blooms. This reinforces the need for and the nature of patience.

5. Celebrate *small steps* to calm doubts, remember progress made, and support the next steps to take.

6. Persistence will help you recognize your mistakes and get you through, over, or around them.

7. Long-term calls for patience in the short term.

ASK YOURSELF

- ➤ What would you add to this list?

- ➤ In what areas could you have been more patient?

- ➤ When has patience in a task, a goal, or a relationship brought you rewards?

- ➤ If you have patience, are you a doctor?

   Patience releases time's pressure in your favor.

YOUR DEFINITION OF WORDS

"Words are, of course, the most powerful
drug used by mankind."
—**Rudyard Kipling**

I know that words mean different things to different people. For example, blue can mean one thing to one person and something totally different to another. Work, music, good food, friends, and so on can have different meanings for the individuals who experience them.

Knowing my words, phrases, and tones are guiding my perspectives, I've thought more about what some words mean to me. Certainly, these definitions and meanings will change over time, yet for me, defining the way I see them has been helpful. It's been a small step in recognizing and seeing more clearly their connection to my thinking and emotions.

Here are a few that seem to come up regularly:

1. **LOVE.** While romantic love often takes the spotlight, there is so much more to love than this. I love pets, family, friends, and simple joys like sunny days and walks on the beach. *So, I'll define love as the attraction to something or someone that creates mutual support. Love is key to enjoying more.*

2. **FUN.** I love fun. My parting salutation for years was "Have Fun," and while I didn't think about it much, *I now see fun as **F**orward movement, **U**nweighted, and **N**ow.* If one of the three elements is missing—if you're moving backward, weighed down, or dwelling on the past—it stops being fun. *Having fun and being less serious opens many doors.*

3. **SUCCESS.** Success is measured with many metrics. *I've chosen to view success not as something to wait for but as the simple act of recognizing that each step is a success, building energy and momentum that leads to the next step. Success is feeling the enjoyment of progress.*

4. **HAPPINESS.** My definition of happiness was shared with me by a monk on the side of a mountain as I was trekking in the Himalayas. He said (through a translator) that it was *the simple joy of drinking water, resting when tired, and staying positive.* I also find happiness in moments that make me smile. *Happiness can be found in love, fun, and success.*

Your Definition Of Words

5. **SHIT and FUCK.** Some define these as "inappropriate" words. *I define them and their derivatives as useful in expressing emotions.*

ASK YOURSELF

- ➤ Have you defined the words that are important to you?
- ➤ Has it helped you notice and enjoy more?
- ➤ Could it?

YOU CAN STOP WARRING WITH YOURSELF

> "You, as much as anybody in the entire universe, deserve your love and affection."
> **—Buddha**

Within us, a dialogue between opposing selves constantly plays out in the form of self-kindness and self-criticism. Each side has its place in personal growth, but striking the right balance is the key to well-being. Too much self-kindness without accountability can stall progress, while unchecked self-criticism can drain confidence and motivation.

Self-criticism, commonly called negative self-talk, is your inner troublemaker. Putting yourself down, focusing on your flaws, and avoiding challenges and opportunities because you believe you can't do it are all forms of self-criticism. Self-criticism focuses on your shortcomings, continually pointing out what's wrong or what you could have done better. It can magnify your errors, making you feel that every misstep is a sign of weakness.

Continued self-criticism can create a cycle of low self-esteem and doubt. You no longer recognize progress or achievements; instead, you focus on what's missing or imperfect and things that make you feel like you're not enough.

In contrast, self-kindness, also known as positive self-talk, is your inner ally. It acknowledges your strengths and accomplishments, embraces your imperfections and flaws, and treats you with understanding and forgiveness. It knows that growth and resilience take time and gives you the space to grow at your own pace. It offers encouragement when you need it most and lifts you when things get tough.

Self-kindness doesn't hold grudges and allows you to forgive yourself for past mistakes and move forward with compassion. It recognizes and celebrates *small-step* wins, giving you confidence that makes future challenges feel more manageable.

Positive and negative self-talk don't exist independently. They are parts of everyday perspectives, and sometimes, one is up and the other down.

To break the habit of negative self-talk, start by simply noticing when it happens. Then, counter it not by resisting it but by acknowledging it and overwriting it with self-kindness and positive self-talk.

With awareness and practice, you can change the dialogue, little by little, to one of self-kindness. In turn, you'll feel better about yourself and enjoy more of what you have.

TIPS FOR SELF-KINDNESS

- When your thoughts become overly critical, don't judge—just recognize them.
- When your critical voice starts putting you down, challenge it in the moment.
- Reframe negatives into positives—and criticisms into lessons.
- If there are people who put you down or make you feel less—see them less.
- Prioritize your well-being daily.
- Celebrate your small wins daily.
- Being kind to others will help you be kinder toward yourself.
- Use the practices of BIT, PTR, W4G, and TFM to support your self-kindness.

ASK YOURSELF

- Which inner dialogue do you think you hear the most?
- Are you kind and generous enough to yourself?

Enjoy Today

- If so, great.
- If not, would you like to change the script?

> "Self-kindness is not about
> making yourself positive.
> Rather, it's about not being your critic
> and becoming your cheerleader."

YOU BEING YOU IS THE BEST

Be you—the world will adjust.

You are you—that is a fundamental truth of life.

Being you—that is a fundamental strength of life.

But which you should you be?

Easy: Be the one you'd be proud of.

- ➢ Do you know this?
- ➢ Are you doing what excites, challenges, or feels right for you?
- ➢ Are you making space for yourself?

In a world of expectations, there is no single way to be you. It's easy to get caught up in being what others need or want you to be. There's nothing wrong with prioritizing others; many times, others rightly take center stage. Working with others and their priorities is often necessary when you have children, family, friends, teams, and careers. It can allow you to enjoy more and learn lessons, including empathy, compromise, and the strength of good relationships.

But no matter the task, role, or moment, it's worth considering that by honestly sharing your thoughts and feelings with others, you bring the best to the table for everyone—and in the end, that strengthens you and those you're supporting.

> "Until I believe in myself—nobody else will."
> **—Jack Canfield**

Being honest about your feelings, likes, and dislikes is a skill, and like any skill, it improves with practice. *Small steps* will help you grow in this honesty, and you'll enjoy more of what you have because you're being more of who you are. In doing so, you'll cultivate and unlock potent abilities. The power to say no becomes a superpower, and knowing when to say yes enlightens your day.

Countless philosophers, writers, and educators have explored this theme. They argue that being who you are leads to greater enjoyment, self-acceptance, and stronger connections with others. I share many of these quotes here because their insights remain timeless and worth revisiting:

> "The worst loneliness is not to be comfortable with yourself."
> **—Mark Twain**

You Being You Is The Best

"Be yourself; everyone else is already taken."
—Oscar Wilde

"To be yourself in a world that is constantly trying to make you something else; is the greatest accomplishment."
—Ralph Waldo Emerson

"Be who you are and say what you feel because those who mind don't matter, and those who matter don't mind."
—Bernard M. Baruch

"The individual has always had to struggle to keep from being overwhelmed by the tribe."
—Friedrich Nietzsche

"You are not a drop in the ocean. You are the entire ocean in a drop."
—Rumi

"Don't compromise yourself. You're all you've got."
—Janis Joplin

"To find yourself, think for yourself."
—Socrates

Enjoy Today

"The question isn't who you'll be in the future. The question is who you are becoming right now."
—Oprah Winfrey

"Your time is limited, so don't waste it living someone else's life."
—Steve Jobs

"The privilege of a lifetime is to become who you truly are."
—Carl Jung

BEGIN—TO ENJOY TODAY

"The perfect moment to start is when you realize there is no perfect moment."

Some will begin to Enjoy Today because they want to add something meaningful to their life, and that's great.

Others may never begin to Enjoy Today because they're content with how things are or believe that change isn't possible. And that's perfectly fine, too.

The truth is, Enjoy Today is always available whenever you are ready—whether to help you enjoy more or to pursue more of what you truly desire.

The steps and practices you'll find here offer a wealth of benefits, but no one can tell you the exact moment to start applying them to your life. That decision belongs to you—the one who will harness their power.

Many have found that the practices I've outlined—TOSSLY Flow Meditation (TFM), See the Best in Today (BIT), Writing 4

Enjoy Today

Growth (W4G), and Pausing to Refresh (PTR)—are effective *small steps* to help you focus on enjoying today, and today is the basis on which everything else will be built.

> "Begin before you're ready.
> Readiness is a myth that keeps
> dreams dormant."

CONCLUSION

You are you.
And will always be.

The steps you take are yours to take.

If you're still here and hearing this rhyme,
I thank you greatly for taking the time.

In support of you and the steps you choose . . .

I send you best wishes,
I send you strength,
I send you prayers.

So without dwelling on more to say,
I sincerely hope you Enjoy Today.

GLOSSARY OF TERMS

ARC of life

A personal storyline that has a beginning, a middle, and an end, in which you are the main character. Over time, its stages and phases significantly influence a plot where you develop and/or decline.

BIT (See the Best in Today)

A practice that helps you notice and build upon the good things in your day that may otherwise have gone unnoticed. In a few intentional moments, you think about your day's best moments and write them down. Over time, you'll start to notice things you previously overlooked.

ENJOY

To take pleasure or find satisfaction in something, whether it's an activity or an experience. It often involves a sense of happiness, appreciation, or contentment in the moment and is frequently accompanied by a slight smile.

ENJOY TODAY

To Enjoy Today is not about forgetting yesterday, settling, or giving up on tomorrow. Instead, it's about appreciating the power of today, this one day, and letting it fuel a greater sense of contentment and purpose. It is also this book you are reading right now.

"GROWING UP VOICES"

The voices that combined as you were learning to be "yourself." Whether quiet or loud, optimistic or pessimistic, they influenced you with the needs and views of others that may still affect you today.

PROBLEM

A tangible challenge that can range from frustrating and sad to overwhelming and painful, and that requires a solution.

PTR (Pausing To REfresh)

A practice that offers an effective way to rethink priorities, manage stress, enhance focus, or rejuvenate at any time during the day. Also, the practice for harnessing the power of REwords.

REwords

Words that, when used intentionally, allow you to stop, breathe, and take another look at your progress. They encourage mindfulness and help you appreciate where you are rather than being stuck where you think you should be. Such words include

REst, REthink, REview, REcharge, REimagine, REstore, Reframe, and REfocus.

SMALL STEPS

Falling in love, having kids, or building a home, a business, or a career doesn't happen overnight. It's always about the often unnoticed *small steps* that move you closer to what you want— to accept a challenge, to overcome it, and to learn from it. Big achievements and lasting relationships may steal the spotlight, but the real work, the real magic, is in the *small steps* that move you toward what you desire.

TFM (TOSSLY Flow Meditation)

A versatile self-guided practice to recognize, guide, and support your thoughts and feelings, regularly and as they surface throughout the day.

TODAY

The current day—the twenty-four-hour period in which you are presently living. It represents the time between yesterday and tomorrow. It, and only it, provides the opportunity for action, reflection, and personal change.

TOSSLY (Truth Of Small Steps— Lead Yourself)

Truth reflects accuracy, authenticity, and reliability.

Small steps connect you with your moments and the now of your life, reminding you to live fully—not someday, but right now.

Lead Yourself (it has also been *Love Yourself*) gives you the power of self-direction.

TRUE SELF

The most authentic, unfiltered version of you—free from the weight of societal expectations, fears, and the roles you are obligated to play.

TRUE-SELF PROBLEMS

Unlike traditional problems, true-self problems reside in your thoughts and emotions. They are deeply individual yet surprisingly universal and can repeat on an endless loop, lingering as worry and stress, influencing your decisions, lifestyle, and interactions with the world.

VOICES OF OTHERS

"Voices" belonging to other people that are unconcerned about appreciating your uniqueness and how you could enjoy yourself. They make you forget to pause, ask yourself what you truly enjoy, and listen to your answers.

W4G (Writing 4 Growth)

A transformative practice and way of writing to bring order and understanding to your thoughts, clarify your perspectives, and guide your *small steps* in the directions you choose.

WORRIES

The anticipation of negative outcomes, whether or not they actually happen. Worries create stress and test your resilience, adaptability, and inner strength.

LIST OF QUOTATIONS

"Life isn't easy—get used to it."
—Bill Gates

There's a lot of shit out there.

Ours is such a short moment on this earth; don't let the good bits pass you by.

"Enjoy life. There's plenty of time to be dead."
—Hans Christian Andersen

"The past is unchangeable, and the future is uncertain. Therefore, our focus should be on making the most of today."
—John Wooden

Enjoy Today

"The best way to pay for a lovely moment
is to enjoy it."
—Richard Bach

"Enjoy the little things, for one day you may look
back and realize they were the big things."
—Robert Brault

Choice, a whispered path. One step sets the
journey's course. Destiny unfolds.

"The music is not in the notes,
but in the silence between."
—Wolfgang Amadeus Mozart

Pause for rethinking.
Reset for resilience.
Reimagine during times of transition.

"Almost everything will work again if you
unplug it for a few minutes, including you."
—Anne Lamott

"You are alive today, and that's enough reason
to celebrate and make the most of it."
—Orison Swett Marden

List Of Quotations

"Don't count the days; make the days count."
—Muhammad Ali

"Today is life—the only life you are sure of.
Make the most of today."
—Dale Carnegie

Use a meditation that becomes part of you—
as you become a better you.

"Don't curse the darkness; light a candle."
—Chinese Proverb

W4G literally gives you another perspective
of what you're thinking.

"The mind is not a vessel to be filled,
but a fire to be kindled."
—Plutarch

Thinking is nonsense, and writing
makes sense of it.

Think of W4G as a conversation
with yourself on paper.

Listening to others is important;
listening to yourself is enlightening.

Enjoy Today

"You have brains in your head. You have feet in your shoes. You can steer yourself in any direction you choose."
—Dr. Seuss

"Logic will get you from A to B. Imagination will take you everywhere."
—Albert Einstein

"If you know where you're going, every step has purpose."
—Zig Ziglar

Personal vulnerability is easier when it's private.

"I have self-doubt. I have insecurity. I have a fear of failure."
—Kobe Bryant

"Great things are not done by impulse, but by a series of small things brought together."
—Vincent Van Gogh

"Time is a created thing. To say 'I don't have time' is to say 'I don't want to.'"
—Lao Tzu

List Of Quotations

"The greatest mistake you can make is continually fearing you will make one."
—Elbert Hubbard

"The blank page is not empty, it's filled with the honesty of having nothing to say."

You may not remember your way, but you can find it. It's there for you.

"You have power over your mind, not outside events. Realize this, and you will find strength."
—Marcus Aurelius

Thinking is using your mind and giving thought a chance.

"An open mind leaves a chance for someone to drop a worthwhile thought in it."
—Mark Twain

"The mind is like a parachute. It doesn't work if it is not open."
—Frank Zappa

"Having options is the foundation of autonomy and self-determination."
—**Malcolm Gladwell**

Think more about what you want—and less about what you don't want.

"Focus is a matter of deciding what things you're not going to do."
—**John Carmack**

"The capacity to learn is a gift; the ability to learn is a skill; the willingness to learn is a choice."
—**Brian Herbert**

"The most difficult part of adult learning is choosing to learn."
—**Seth Godin**

"Your body is an instrument, not an ornament."
—**Unknown**

"When the breath is steady and controlled, the mind is still and calm."
—**B.K.S. Iyengar**

List Of Quotations

A body at rest tends to stay at rest. A body in motion tends to stay in motion.

"Let's not forget that the little emotions are the great captains of our lives, and we obey them without realizing it."
—Vincent Van Gogh

Emotions are you connecting with your heart.

Acknowledging emotions validates your experiences, reinforcing that your feelings are real and worthy of attention.

"It's intriguing; when I acknowledge myself just as I am, I can change."
—Carl Rogers

"When we clarify our emotions, we are no longer at their mercy. We become empowered to choose how to move forward."
—Susan David

"Feelings are much like waves; we can't stop them from coming, but we can choose which one to surf."
—Jonatan Mårtensson

"There is a force in the universe, which, if we permit it, will flow through us and produce miraculous results."
—Mahatma Gandhi

"Be thankful for what you have; and you'll end up having more. If you focus on what you don't have, you'll never have enough."
—Oprah Winfrey

With a grateful heart, you will attract more of what you are grateful for.

"You don't have to be an angel to act like one."
—Mort Schapiro

"We make a living by what we get, but we make a life by what we give."
—Winston Churchill

"A belief is not merely an idea the mind possesses; it is an idea that possesses the mind."
—Robert Oxton Bolton

"Faith is a knowledge within the heart, beyond the reach of proof."
—Kahlil Gibran

List Of Quotations

"To forgive is to set a prisoner free and discover that the prisoner was you."
—Lewis B. Smedes

Everything worthwhile takes time. Often more time than expected.

If you had yesterday to do over (you don't), how would you apply that to today?

Priorities aren't just what we list. They're actually what we do, choose, and invest our time in daily.

"The key is not to prioritize what's on your schedule, but to schedule your priorities."
—Stephen Covey

Practice when the stakes are low—to be prepared when the stakes are high.

"Practice is the best of all instructors."
—Publilius Syrus

"A river cuts through rock, not because of its power, but because of its persistence."
—James N. Watkins

Enjoy Today

"It's not that I'm so smart; it's just that I stay with problems longer."
—Albert Einstein

"Everything takes time—many times more time than you think."
—Morgan Harper Nichols

Overnight success is a myth.

Patience releases time's pressure in your favor.

Small steps are a process, not a miracle.

The truth of moving forward is to get started.
The truth to getting started is *small steps*.
The truth of making progress is to keep going.
The truth to keep going is *small steps*.

"A step back from the wrong direction is a step in the right direction."
—Scott Galloway

List Of Quotations

When you take the easy ones,
the tough ones become easier.
"You don't have to see the whole staircase; just take the first step."
—Martin Luther King Jr.

"The most important conversations you'll ever have is the one you have with yourself."
—David Goggins

Perspective leads to self-talk. Self-talk shapes your perspective.

The truth of personal perspective is clear . . .
You are the only person who can change yours.

"Today, I will see more of what I want and less of what I don't want."
—Abraham Hicks

What you see is what you get—
or stay away from.

To reach the peaks, you have to
go through valleys.

Enjoy Today

"The middle is messy, but it's also where the magic happens."
—**Brené Brown**

When you are ready, the beginning will appear.

"The beginning is the most important part of the work."
—**Plato**

You may be in the middle of a chapter, but you can always start a new one.

"Words are the most powerful force available to humanity."
—**Yehuda Berg**

Today, I will tell myself more of what I enjoy and less of what I don't like.

"Words are free; how you use them may cost you."
—**Kushandwizdom**

"Words are, of course, the most powerful drug used by mankind."
—**Rudyard Kipling**

List Of Quotations

"You, as much as anybody in the entire universe, deserve your love and affection."
—Buddha

Self-kindness is not about making yourself positive.
Rather, it's about not being your critic and becoming your cheerleader.

Be you—the world will adjust.

"Until I believe in myself—nobody else will."
—Jack Canfield

The power to say NO will become a superpower, and saying YES will feel so much better.

"The worst loneliness is not to be comfortable with yourself."
—Mark Twain

"Be yourself; everyone else is already taken."
—Oscar Wilde

"To be yourself in a world that is constantly trying to make you something else; is the greatest accomplishment."
—Ralph Waldo Emerson

"Be who you are and say what you feel because those who mind don't matter, and those who matter don't mind."
—Bernard M. Baruch

"The individual has always had to struggle to keep from being overwhelmed by the tribe."
—Friedrich Nietzsche

"You are not a drop in the ocean. You are the entire ocean in a drop."
—Rumi

"Don't compromise yourself. You're all you've got."
—Janis Joplin

"To find yourself, think for yourself."
—Socrates

"The question isn't who you'll be in the future. The question is who you are becoming right now."
—Oprah Winfrey

"Your time is limited, so don't waste it living someone else's life."
—Steve Jobs

"The privilege of a lifetime is to become who you truly are."
—Carl Jung

The perfect moment to start is when you realize there is no perfect moment.

Begin before you're ready.
Readiness is a myth that keeps dreams dormant.

"Alone, we can do so little; together, we can do so much. Be thankful for those who lift you up."
—Helen Keller

Enjoy Today

Thank you to my family for creating me.
Thank you to my people for shaping me.
Thank you to the greats for inspiring me.
Thank you to you for reading me.
—Luke B. Greenwood

ACKNOWLEDGEMENTS

"Alone, we can do so little; together, we can do so much. Be thankful for those who lift you up."
—**Helen Keller**

I am deeply grateful for the wise words of the famous, those I love, those I have called on, and the amazing shoulders I stand on. Their insights have shaped much of what I share here.

Each individual will interpret and apply these TOSSLY thoughts in their own unique way. There is no one-size-fits-all formula—these ideas are intended to inspire, not dictate.

The goal is to highlight the power of *small steps* and the importance of today and the moments we take to act. However, the truth is that everyone will use this information differently, developing and prioritizing what resonates most with them.

Many excellent resources are available to guide you in what to do and how to do it. Listen to the ones that speak to you and make sense of your journey.

Enjoy Today

I appreciate the time you have given to these writings and hope they have helped you enjoy more of what you have. We are lucky to have life's opportunities.

> Thank you to my family for creating me.
> Thank you to my people for shaping me.
> Thank you to the greats for inspiring me.
> Thank you to you for reading me.
> **—Luke B. Greenwood**

ABOUT JG

"In my defense, I have none."
—Taylor Swift

I was born into a middle-class family.

Into a family that cared for me.

Into a generation that worked for me: the baby boom.

Looking back on my life, I realize that becoming who I am today was a process of not knowing what to do and then doing something. Second-guessing that I could until I found myself doing it. The one common thread that bound it all together was personal change.

I grew up in the postwar boom years in Long Beach, California. It was known as "Iowa by the sea," a mix of midwestern solidity and possibility blowing in from nearby Los Angeles. I grew up in what, to me, was a loving home, and I worked odd jobs before graduating from the University of Southern California with degrees in finance and sociology. I had been on course to become a lawyer, but I realized that lawyers spend all their time dealing with other people's problems. I wanted to make my own.

For my first set of problems, I opened a small record store called Licorice Pizza (think flat, black, and round). One store grew to thirty-six, and this business became the launching pad for other companies and projects. It was also at Licorice Pizza where I met my wife, Patty. I have always loved music, and when I met her for the first time for a job interview, she told me, "For everything, there is a song." I loved that, and it has stuck with me for decades. Patty, too.

After five years of being unable to conceive, we started a family and raised four children to thriving adulthood. To focus on my young family, I took up offers to buy my businesses and stopped working. I found this difficult, as it meant I had to stop defining myself by what I did and start defining myself by who I was. This retirement lasted five years, and though I went back to running businesses and chairing a non-profit, this change of perspective set the foundation for TOSSLY.

After retiring from retirement, I started a business called Profitable Connections. We consulted with small business executives, and a clear pattern struck me: whatever their business talents and successes, they were also interested in finding more time for themselves and their families. While they understood the time commitment required for their careers, they also wanted to be better connected to others, healthier, and enjoy more of life.

ABOUT JG

"In my defense, I have none."
—Taylor Swift

I was born into a middle-class family.

Into a family that cared for me.

Into a generation that worked for me: the baby boom.

Looking back on my life, I realize that becoming who I am today was a process of not knowing what to do and then doing something. Second-guessing that I could until I found myself doing it. The one common thread that bound it all together was personal change.

I grew up in the postwar boom years in Long Beach, California. It was known as "Iowa by the sea," a mix of midwestern solidity and possibility blowing in from nearby Los Angeles. I grew up in what, to me, was a loving home, and I worked odd jobs before graduating from the University of Southern California with degrees in finance and sociology. I had been on course to become a lawyer, but I realized that lawyers spend all their time dealing with other people's problems. I wanted to make my own.

For my first set of problems, I opened a small record store called Licorice Pizza (think flat, black, and round). One store grew to thirty-six, and this business became the launching pad for other companies and projects. It was also at Licorice Pizza where I met my wife, Patty. I have always loved music, and when I met her for the first time for a job interview, she told me, "For everything, there is a song." I loved that, and it has stuck with me for decades. Patty, too.

After five years of being unable to conceive, we started a family and raised four children to thriving adulthood. To focus on my young family, I took up offers to buy my businesses and stopped working. I found this difficult, as it meant I had to stop defining myself by what I did and start defining myself by who I was. This retirement lasted five years, and though I went back to running businesses and chairing a non-profit, this change of perspective set the foundation for TOSSLY.

After retiring from retirement, I started a business called Profitable Connections. We consulted with small business executives, and a clear pattern struck me: whatever their business talents and successes, they were also interested in finding more time for themselves and their families. While they understood the time commitment required for their careers, they also wanted to be better connected to others, healthier, and enjoy more of life.

About JG

Looking around, I found lots of information on business change but very little on personal change. Yes, there was the usual carousel of ideas and instruction for self-improvement in specific areas: to lose weight, shed stress, or find love. But each of these guides was stuck in their deep silo of particular ideas and didn't make the "big picture" link that seemed evident to me: one step at a time is progress.

Around this time, I wanted a more aggressive exercise program. I didn't just want to sweat more; I also wanted to be able to protect myself and my family should I ever have to. Four times a day, I went past a martial arts studio while dropping the kids off at school. One day, I stopped. Looking in, I saw black belts doing moves I admired but never thought I would be capable of. I decided to start anyway.

When I started learning martial arts, I was taught that reaching that black belt was just a series of repeated *small steps*. You practice one thing over and over again. Then, when you've learned it, you practice the next thing over and over and over again. It took six years of these shuffling *small steps*, but I eventually earned my own Black Belt that inspired TOSSLY's middle name: *small steps*.

Together, these experiences gave me simple insights into personal change. *Small steps* gave initiative and effort a way forward and a way to make sense of nonsensical things. I found an effective, efficient way to distill more of what I enjoy and guide changes to more of what I want.

With Enjoy Today, I hope you will find a way, too.

www.ingramcontent.com/pod-product-compliance
Lightning Source LLC
Chambersburg PA
CBHW030453100526
44580CB00009B/113/J